WOMAN STAND FIRM

Armor Up In The Battle For Your Identity

Karen
McCracken

Dedication

This book is for all women who have been told they're not enough, they're too much, they aren't smart enough, they aren't valued and they don't have talent. This book is for every woman who gave away parts of who she is because she thought she had to in order to be loved. This is for every woman, no matter your age, your weight, your size, how much money you have; if you're married, divorced or single, with or without children; that you may come to know, that who you are and who God made you to be, is worth fighting for. This book is for you, every woman, because now is the time to pick up your armor and ready yourself in the battle for your identity.

Thank you to all the strong women of God in my life, past and present, who have been a beautiful example to me.

~ Karen

KAREN MCCRACKEN

Contents

WOMAN STAND FIRM

Introduction

"Be on your guard; stand firm in the faith; be courageous; be strong." ~ **1 Corinthians 16:13**

The Word of God tells us in more than one place that we are to stand firm, stand our ground and be prepared for battle against the darkness that threatens to overtake us. I've had a battle cry on my heart for a long time and my desire has been to share that cry with other women. With that as my goal, I started a podcast in late 2019. Doing a weekly podcast to encourage, educate, and inspire women only added fuel to the fire within me that burns to reach a culture of women whose very identity is being picked away at, attacked, and berated.

I spent too many years of my life wondering why who I was, wasn't good enough. I've spent too many hours wishing my body looked different; praying for God to make me smarter, better, prettier; so I would feel good enough to be obedient to Him and serve where and when He wanted me to without fear. For a long time I allowed my insecurities, pain and self-loathing to keep me from being fully obedient to that call. With every new trend, every year that passed by, every latest cultural craze, I saw myself differently. Defining myself according to what role I was playing at the time; student, wife, mom, daughter, youth pastor, only created confusion as those roles changed over time to divorced, empty-nester, graduate. I had no idea who I truly was. When the reflection I saw in the mirror, and becoming what I thought others expected me to be, became more important than whether or not I reflected God's love, I realized that I had no idea who I truly was. I set out on a journey to find out who I am and that process took me straight back to the only source of truth on the subject; the Word of God.

Every single day women across the globe are hurting, victimized, put down, and told we're not enough or maybe that we're too much. Who we are has become dependent on what social media, changing cultural norms, and the world at large says women should be. Every single day we battle the enemy and the world to retain an identity that is pleasing to as many people as possible. The roles we play, titles we earn and labels others put upon us, as well as the hurt we've endured, have become our identity. It's time to change that.

Within this book I encourage all women to find out the truth of who they are by understanding whose they are. Inside these pages are the words, scripture, personal insights and battle cry to all women - those within the church and those who have yet to know our Lord and Savior. My prayer is that if you do not know Jesus, that the words within will create a thirst and hunger for you to know Him, and to understand that there is power in belonging to the Kingdom of God. Women of

God, I encourage you to pray, read this book with an open heart and mind and get prepared to stand firm.

~ Karen

To find Karen's podcast, go to womaninspired.com or search for The Woman Inspired Podcast in your favorite podcast player

KAREN MCCRACKEN

WHO DO YOU BELIEVE YOURSELF TO BE?

How do you identify yourself? Most of us identify ourselves according to what we do for a living, what our marital status is, whether or not we're a parent; how we look or even what we aspire to be. Perhaps you identify yourself according to what your driver's license says or your marital status, race, height, weight, eye color, address? Are all those physical characteristics and roles you play actually who you are?

I am not what my physical body looks like. I am not a brown-eyed girl. I am a girl who has brown eyes. I am not a 56 year old woman. I am a woman who turned 56 this year. The totality of who I am is not defined by the fact that I'm a wife or a mom. I am a woman who has a role as a wife and is blessed to be married. Am I splicing words and making slight distinctions that truly don't matter? Perhaps the wording doesn't matter as it sits here on the page but when you digest it, take it on as your identity and attempt to walk in that role, that title, the worldly definition of yourself, then, yes it matters immensely. You see, if I say, "I am a wife", and I wrap my identity and purpose in the fact that I am a wife, yet 10 years down the road I find myself widowed or divorced, does that change who I am? Because the truth would then be that I am no longer a wife. I am a widow. Or I am a single woman. If I wrapped my entire identity up in one defining label and that label changes, then who am I? Is life meant to be a series of constant unstable definitions of who I am? Am I supposed to forever be on some hippy style, 60's trek to find myself? No, I'm not, and neither are you. This is why defining ourselves according to titles, labels, and roles, is not only false, but harmful.

Who you believe yourself to be can change how you think, how you react to challenges in life and whether or not you're obedient to God. You are not what has happened to you. You are not the mistakes you've made, or the sins you've committed. You are not the ailments that you have or the disease that plagues you. If you're operating from a belief that you are those things and the experiences, mistakes, sins and tragedies in your life define you, then you are allowing the world's ideas of what is valuable and who is valuable, guide your daily decisions.

Since the beginning of time the world has placed certain value on various aspects of life. Satan uses those worldly values, stereo-types and judgments to keep us questioning ourselves, and reminding us that we have little to no value in this world. But Satan is a liar and when we fall for the world's idea of who and what is valuable, we miss the opportunity to walk in the truth and power of who we truly are, and often times end up wallowing in the identity of someone we were never born to be.

The Bible tells about a Samaritan woman who came to the well one day to draw water. (**John 4:5-30**) This woman was a social outcast. She had been married 5 times and was living with a man at this time. She was unmarried and had a sketchy reputation. She was at the well near the hottest time of the day, which was unusual for someone gathering water. Typically the women would go get water from the well early in the morning in order to stay out of the heat. She came at a time when no one else would be at the well because she was scorned and looked down upon. She didn't know she would encounter Jesus that day. As you read in John 4 you will come to see as the Samaritan woman did that Jesus reveals himself to her. He doesn't condemn her, though He knows she is living with a man she is not married to and she has been married 5 times. While other people condemned her, Jesus did not. Her sin is still her sin but Jesus asks her for water, even though the rest of the people wouldn't dare to do such a thing. Jesus ends up saying to her: **John 4:13-14**, "[13] Everyone who drinks this water will be thirsty again, [14] but whoever drinks the water I give them will never thirst. Indeed, the water I give them will become in them a spring of water welling up to eternal life."

Jesus shared with her that He was the Living Water. She wanted the living water. She wanted to drink from the water that would make her thirst no more. Do you think perhaps she was thirsting for some attention, some love, some fulfillment in all the men she'd had? And all she ended up needing was Jesus. He could quench her thirst once and for all. He wasn't put off or shocked by her sin. He didn't withhold who He was or treat her poorly because of what she had been labeled. Jesus saw her as a woman who needed to know Him. He saw who she was beyond how she identified herself in worldly terms. She saw herself as not good enough to come to the well when other women were coming to the well but after her encounter with Jesus she was unashamed, unhindered and ran into the town to tell everyone about Jesus.

Like the Samaritan woman at the well, we can go to the Lord with the assurance that He came to save us, not condemn us. Jesus waits with open arms for all those who have let the world claim them as their own. We are not of this world though. We belong to Jesus. When we accept who Jesus is, like the woman at the well, we can freely let go of what society thinks we are; of what family members and so-called friends have labeled us due to our past. We can let go of who or what we thought we were and allow Jesus to be our Living Water that we will thirst no more for the things of this world. When we do, we will want to run and tell others about Jesus, just as she did.

Let's look at David from the Bible. You'll find his story in 1st and 2nd Samuel and 1st and 2nd Chronicles. He's likely best known for being the one who used a slingshot to kill a Giant. (David and Goliath). If you looked at David through the eyes of his brother, who treated David as if he was incapable of anything, you would see David as a lowly shepherd boy, yet he became a giant-slayer. God saw David as even more than that. God saw him as a king. David was from the tribe of Judah. He was imperfect and had many flaws but he loved God and had a heart for Him. David grew into a man who became the most important King of Israel. David is an example of a real, imperfect person who was judged by a family member, yet overcame the labels thrust upon him, to become a King.

IDENTITY CRISIS

I've found over the past 20 years in serving the Lord by bringing His message of love, forgiveness, hope and eternal life to women all over the country, that women from every walk of life are affected by an intense wondering - wondering who they are, how they fit in, why they don't fit in; wondering why they're too much or not enough; wondering why they only feel good, confident and loved for a season and then that feeling disappears. This happens with women from every socioeconomic category I've encountered. From poor, widowed, Appalachian mountain ladies living paycheck to paycheck and hand out to hand out, to city slicking, top executives who have a high priced car, stocks and bonds and a closet filled with expensive high heels. Identity issues know NO bounds. The wondering who, how, why, and what you're going to do about it, is not relegated to one type of woman. It's not only the women who are outside the Body of Christ but many inside the Body of Christ who faithfully attend a church, go to Bible study, and listen to contemporary Christian music.

The fact is, through ministering to women of all walks, vocations, ages and stages; I have seen that the identity crisis that has swept across culture is just that, a true crisis. We are living in a day and age when scores of women (and men) have no idea who they are except for what the world has told them they are or should aspire to be. We have a culture filled with women from teenagers to senior citizens who are thirsting for love, attention and affection that they feel they don't deserve because Satan has told them they don't deserve it. We have a world filled with hurting women who won't go to the well and be seen in public but who are ashamed, sitting behind a screen and a keyboard, seeking attention and trying to figure out who they are.

In a culture that glorifies sin, we have mass numbers of women who are dying inside because they are identifying themselves with the sins that entangle them. Jesus, who poured out His compassion and truth upon the woman at the well, a woman the rest of the world condemned, is here today to do the same for each of us. In order to become to know who we are, we have to accept that we are daughters of the King of Kings, the Lord of Lords. He is the compassionate One who does not hold us to worldly labels. Like David, we have to set aside the names others call us and be willing to step into whatever position God calls us to. We have to be willing, like the woman at the well, to forget about social expectations and definitions, and carry the message of our Savior to the rest of the world. This is what we're called to do. We, who have been chosen by a mighty Father in Heaven, to be His hands and feet, are called to remember that we are daughters of the King of Kings. We are not daughters of a dark and fallen world. And it's imperative we slay the negative, modern day terms and labels we keep speaking over ourselves and others in order to embrace who Jesus says we truly are.

A case of mistaken identity

I read a quote the other day by Thomas Browne that says, "Rough diamonds are often mistaken for worthless pebbles." Is that how they saw Jesus? As a pebble who was just making waves as it was tossed in the pool of other religious icons of the day? He was mocked, arrested, beaten, spit on, stoned and crucified by most, rather than them understanding that He was a diamond. He was THE diamond - the priceless rock.

According to Miriam Webster, mistaken identity is simply defined as "a situation in which someone or something is mistakenly thought to be someone or something else." That not only defines how people saw Jesus back in the days he walked on this earth but also how many people still see Him today. They think Jesus was a condemning, preachy, over reaching figure who was prejudice and taught His followers to be the same. Some people mistakenly see him as merely a wise man, a prophet, and a moral figure from days gone by.

Have you ever been looked at differently, judged, called names, or disrespected by someone who thought they knew who you were? They thought that because they could label you as a Christian that they had you pegged? Was it also a case of mistaken identity? Perhaps they mistakenly thought you were someone who walks the earth to act holier than they are. If so, it's usually because someone hasn't taken the time to get to know you or know what you believe, how you live, and who you truly are. They have made an assumption on your identity because they know not what a Christian truly is and who Jesus was and is today.

I wonder how many of us identify ourselves as

one thing but are mistaken because our idea of who we are is ever-changing? Do we also do as others sometimes do and define or identify ourselves as one thing, when we actually are not that thing? How many of us have been told our whole lives that we are ugly, fat, skinny, not good enough, stupid, not smart enough, lazy, not talented? So, we mistakenly have believed it? Our identity became wrapped up in a pocket full of wordy lies that others told us and so, without question, we have taken those words in and believed them. We have used their judgments to label ourselves with the very words that hurt us. We have taken that description of ourselves and wallpapered it over the truth of who we are; so much so that only a very little bit of who God designed us to be is still showing through.

Many of us have taken on the identity the world has given us rather than who we really are. How many of us start something, feeling the desire and calling to do it but never finish, because in our minds and hearts we hear the voices and see the faces of people who told us we were not capable? We hear the continual rhetoric that we couldn't accomplish much because we are too timid, too lazy, not smart enough, and not talented enough? And maybe worse yet, how many of us have strived to live up to and recreate ourselves in to the image of what we mistakenly think our identity should be according to what the world says we should be? Sexier, thinner, wealthier, stronger. It's almost like culture has convinced women that we must have a constant identity make over.

If you look around at the largest form of communication and media today, social media, it's no wonder. We are assaulted with images of what and who an "ideal woman" is and being told that if we are not good enough to be a woman, we can always become a man. Women in numbers too large to count, of all walks of life, including women of God, have gone to photo-shopping and filtering their identities to make themselves look better to the world at large. The truth is that who God made us to be...who God made YOU to be, is far better than any image the world could lead you to morph yourself into. Who you are is determined by who God calls you to be, who He made you to be, who He is calling you to become, not who the world says you should be and certainly not who social media lures you to become.

The trend today is the 'perfect mom', connoisseur of stylish clothing, fashion icon, make up wearing, fit and fab, socially appropriate, politically correct, woman of the world who is submissive to the beck and call of societies ideas of what and who she should be today. Believe me when I tell this to you, Woman of God, who the world says you should be today will likely change by next week and next year and the year after when all the while, your identity should not be up for sale to the highest bidder with the most likes and follows on social media.

Being the consistent, child of God you were made to be, standing firm, on a solid foundation that doesn't shake and crumble when the world around us does, is a necessity. Satan is roaming around, prowling for women weakened by the hurt of mistaken identity. He wants you to morph and change with the world's ever changing morals and cultural norms. The enemy wants you to value what the world says is important today, tomorrow and the next day rather than valuing who God says you are today and for eternity. The world will tell us that who we are totally depends on who we are willing to please and who we are willing to change for so we can be accepted, revered and adored by them. But who we are should only be based on who we are in Christ, not by who wants to own us, pay us, judge us, or momentarily tell us they value us. Our worth is based in the reality of not just who we are but WHOSE we are.

Part of the reason we are in battle against the one who wishes to seek and destroy our identity is because the world at large has been led by evil into having a total case of illogical, unspiritual, self-guided definition of who and what people should be. What do I mean by that?

Let's look at this short, simple quote by Leo Tolstoy. "What a strange illusion it is to suppose that beauty is goodness." When I read that I thought, "Aha, there it is. There is the essence of truth and the very deception that Satan uses to beguile women and men into believing that who we are is not enough." When society and the world at large looks at a person and judges him or her according to the attributes they find attractive in the moment and labels that person as good or bad, worthy or unworthy, merely because of those societal definitions of beauty and goodness, then that is where mistaken identity becomes the enemy's weapon of choice.

When we suppose that what is outside is all that matters; when we look not at the fruit a tree bears but how beautiful, ornate or leafy it is instead of at the hardiness and goodness of the tree and what purpose it might fulfill, we have just mistakenly identified the tree as good, without truly knowing it's good. We have then identified a tree for its beauty alone rather than for the quality of the tree and its fruit. When anyone one looks at a man or woman and decides how good he or she must be according to how good they look in the moment, judging him or her according to the current cultural definition of beautiful, then we have just assumed, like Tolstoy said, that physical beauty is goodness.

There are some beautiful trees along the edge of

my property. I wanted to dig them up this past spring while they were small and replant them in my front yard because they're gorgeous when they bloom. I have no idea what kind they are. They look similar to a cherry tree, though they don't bear any fruit. So, as we went to dig them up we got really close and found out the hard way that they are filled with very sharp thorns. They had so many thorns that there was no way we could handle them to transplant them. I used to believe that tree was the best tree in my yard because of how beautiful it was. Reality hit me when I realized the damage the non-fruit bearing tree could do. I realized I needed to embrace the older, not as pretty, large, hardy tree in my side yard that bears walnuts. It's the better tree. It bears fruit and one day can be used to build something strong that will last for many years to come.

What I want you to understand is what God put on my heart here - that the world is filled with cases of accidental, non-intentional mistaken identity, but be aware that it is also filled with purposeful, callous, evil-hearted cases of orchestrated mistaken identity. Sadly, we live at a time when those within the church and outside the church are living oblivious to the fact that we are in a very real spiritual battle for our identity. So many women have no idea what their own identity is because they're listening to the world and what the world says about them. Christians and non-Christians alike are being attacked with confusion, deception, and distraction designed by the enemy to keep us from knowing that we are not of this world and we are who God says we are, not who the world says we are.

What does the Bible say about who you are?

No matter the circumstances under which you were born, God knew it was going to happen. You may seem like an accident to your parents and your relatives may joke that you were totally unexpected but you are not an accident to God: **Psalm 139:13 -16** tells us that "we were formed in the womb. God took the time to knit us together." And if you've ever seen a picture of DNA you know that DNA looks like someone literally took yarn and knitted something. You are not an "oops" or a mistake, no matter what anyone might have told you.

"You are God's temple and His spirit is within you." - **1 Corinthians 3**

Ephesians 2:10 says, "We are His workmanship, created for good works that God prepared for us already!" So, when you feel as if you have no purpose, dismiss that lie. Get rid of it. The Bible tells us plainly that each of us has a purpose as long as we have breath.

"And it is God who establishes us in Christ and He has anointed us, put His seal on us and given us His Spirit in our hearts as His guarantee." - **2 Corinthians 1 21-22**.

Psalm 139: 1-5 says: "You have searched me, LORD, and you know me. [2] You know when I sit and when I rise; you perceive my thoughts from afar. [3] You discern my going out and my lying down; you are familiar with all my ways. [4] Before a word is on my tongue you, LORD, know it completely. [5] You hem me in behind and before me, and you lay your hand upon me."

Now, do you think the God who took the time to create the heavens and the earth doesn't know you? Doesn't know WHO you are? That He would waste a second of His omnipotence, His passion and love on something or someone He doesn't know and who doesn't matter? I don't. I don't think for one second that who the world says you are and mistakenly identifies you as, is truthful and just as importantly, it doesn't matter what the world says you are. It matters who God says you are!

KAREN MCCRACKEN

CHANGING WHAT YOU BELIEVE ABOUT WHO YOU ARE

Do you find yourself, outwardly or perhaps inwardly where no one else can hear you, calling yourself any of the following?

stupid	stubborn
ugly	victim
fat	abused
idiotic	unintelligent
lazy	useless
not enough	untalented
too much	witch (yea, with a B.)
weak	incapable
addict	loser
alcoholic	too skinny

Are you seeing yourself through the eyes of any past or present sins?

sleeping around	adulterer
emotional affairs	liar
sexual affairs	abuser
glutonous	user
murderer	thief
violent	manipulator

In this quest to change your beliefs about who you are, you'll need to call out and condemn those false and negative things you identify yourself as. There are no trustworthy worldly definitions and titles that fit any of us because who we are can only be defined by our Creator. Though it's difficult and perhaps hard to wrap your mind around, there are no adjectives or definitions the world has that you can apply to yourself because who you are is not defined by the world. You identity should be taken straight from the Word of God and who He says you are.

John Piper says, "At the heart of what it means to be a Christian, means to receive a new identity. In Jesus we do not lose our true selves, but we become our true selves, only in Him."

There is only One who has the authority to define you and that is the One who made you. Only our Creator, our Heavenly Father has the right and the power to tell you who you are. When you allow the world to define you and tell you that you are ABC or D then you have just submitted yourself to the authority of the world and the authority of darkness. When Satan whispers in your ear that you are not anything but a sinner and you will never be anything but a sinner, then my hope and prayer for you is that you can declare out loud, "I may be a sinner but I am a sinner who has been saved." The prince of darkness does not have the authority to tell you who you are. When you are a child of God, you are part of the royal priesthood. That means you are redeemed. You are saved. You are victorious; you are not an accident, you are not the scars that you wear; you are not the clothes that you put on or the color of your hair. You are who He says you are because only the One who created you is allowed to define you

I am someone who has a rare connective tissue disorder called Vascular Ehlers Danlos Syndrome (VEDS) but it does not define who I am. I am someone who's been used, who's been forgotten, taken for granted, taken advantage of, and treated poorly at times in my life. But those things can not define me. They used to. When I let those things become who I am and how I make decisions, I separated myself from the Lord because I was being obedient to the definitions of who the world saw me as and how I felt in any given season rather than to the Lord and His call on my life. I had to call these false names out, release them and allow God to show me who I am.

Those names and definitions are things I've been through and still go through but I am not defined by the ice pack or the brace and the walker or all the other things I have to use at times because of the VEDS. I am not defined by the daily pain. That's all part of the journey but it's not who I am. Those things that happen to my body and the tools I use to hold my joints together are part of my life. They are not who I am. I could easily sit in a pity party, taking on the label of a disabled person and let everyone know not to expect much of me, physically, emotionally, or mentally. Sadly, that's what some people in our world today who are considered disabled end up doing. They buy into the rhetoric and negative talk that they are worthless and unable. Disabled does not mean incapable. It means, unable to do certain things, not everything. I have met so many amazing people with various diagnoses and disabilities that are vibrant, capable, intelligent people who are gifted and love the Lord. Who they are is not defined by what they use to help them overcome and manage the flaws in their flesh. These labels are just experiences that I, as well as others, have experienced and walked through, but they cannot define who we are.

Often times I feel as if the things I've been through and that I've walked through, have felt like walking through the fire. Jesus is with me through the fire just like he was with Shadrach, Meshach, and Abednego in the burning fiery furnace. (**Daniel 3:8-25**) Other times I feel as if I am Daniel and these things are the lion. I'm in the den. But God sent angels to close the mouth of the lion and saved Daniel. I had to pray for God to close the mouths of those who use words to try to devour who I am in Christ. Because, like many of us, I am susceptible to believing the lies, manipulation and mean-spirited words that come from other people, I have to seek God for His protection just like Daniel did in the lion's den. These negative things that others say or that I say about myself, are not who I am. If I am truly a child of God, then those things cannot be how I define myself. What you've said and done, what physical challenges you face, the relationships you have, and how successful you are or aren't according to the world, should not be how you define yourself either.

Who should you believe you are?

Again, there is only One who has the authority to define you and that is the One who made you. The Lord knows you better than you even know yourself. You fit with Him. You are not an accident no matter what anyone ever told you or how they made you feel. You deserve to be filled with the One who designed you. When you thirst and hunger for validation, acknowledgement and love, go directly to the One who made you and who knows you. Go to Him in prayer and open The Word of God.

The Word of God is filled with truth, affirmation of who we are, and how God knows us. These are just a small portion of the scriptures that tell us who God made us to be and assure us that He, as our Creator, Savior, maker, Heavenly Father, knows each of us and cares for us.

The Lord knows you

Psalm 139: 1-3 says, "¹You have searched me, LORD, and you know me. ² You know when I sit and when I rise; you perceive my thoughts from afar. ³ You discern my going out and my lying down; you are familiar with all my ways."

Matthew 10: 29- 31 tells you that He cares for you: "²⁹ are not two sparrows sold for a penny? Yet not one of them will fall to the ground outside your Father's care. ³⁰ And even the very hairs of your head are all numbered. ³¹ So don't be afraid; you are worth more than many sparrows."

Genesis 1:27, "[27] So God created mankind in his own image; in the image of God he created them; male and female he created them."

Acts 17:26, "[26] From one man he made all the nations, that they should inhabit the whole earth; and he marked out their appointed times in history and the boundaries of their lands."

Acts: 17:28, "[28] 'For in him we live and move and have our being. As some of your own poets have said, 'We are his offspring.''"

He knows who you are

You are chosen: "[4] For we know, brothers and sisters loved by God, that he has chosen you," - **1 Thessalonians 1:4** and then **Ephesians 1:11-12** says, "[11] In him we were also chosen, having been predestined according to the plan of him who works out everything in conformity with the purpose of his will, [12] in order that we, who were the first to put our hope in Christ, might be for the praise of his glory."

With Him you are strong: "[3] I can do all this through him who gives me strength." **Philippians 4:13**

He has made you beautiful: [11] He has made everything beautiful in its time. He has also set eternity in the human heart; yet no one can fathom what God has done from beginning to end." **Ecclesiastes 3:11**

You are wonderfully made: "[14]I praise you because I am fearfully and wonderfully made; your works are wonderful, I know that full well." **Psalm139:14**

You are a conqueror: "[37] No, in all these things we are more than conquerors through him who loved us." - **Romans 8:37**

You were planned. Your days here are not a mistake: "[16] Your eyes saw my unformed body; all the days ordained for me were written in your book before one of them came to be." - **Psalm 139:16**

THE BATTLE FOR YOUR IDENTITY

Do you know what identity actually is? It's defined by Miriam Webster as "the distinguishing characteristic or personality of an individual."

It's clear to see from the definition that identity is not something you can achieve. It is something you are that distinguishes you from other individuals. It is not defined as something you do, something that's been done to you, something you're accused of, or how you look. It is not something you earn. No, it is not something you can achieve. It is something you receive. If it were something you achieved then with your next mistake or failure, triumph or promotion, your identity would be gone and you would be starting over from scratch trying to figure out who you are. Thankfully your true identity is not something you work to become. It is something you have been given. The only one you can receive it from is the One who made you.

Everyday there is a battle going on in the lives of every man, woman, and child in this world. There is an enemy who wishes to steal your identity. Perhaps steal is the wrong word though because no one can take it from you and keep it for themselves. What the enemy wants more than anything is for you to be confused about your identity and have you declare yourself to be something you're not. The battle for your identity is real. Very real. Every which way we turn there is something or someone attempting to label us, diminish us, push us down, and tell us who we should or shouldn't be and what we are and what we are not, according to our human flaws or imperfections. All these lies are wrapped in pretty packaging by the standards of the world, not Godly standards and expectations.

In this season and time, a war has been specifically waged against the women of the world. Men are being lulled and deceived into believing they can take on the identity of women and women are being coerced into believing they can be men. But the Bible has something to say about how each of us was formed and who we are. That truth contradicts today's cultural viewpoint.

Psalm 139:15-16 says "[15]My frame was not hidden from you when I was made in the secret place, when I was woven together in the depths of the earth. [16] Your eyes saw my unformed body; all the days ordained for me were written in your book before one of them came to be."

God didn't make a mistake when He formed you, or me or anyone. Within His design is a perfect plan for each of us. He has ordained each of us to be who we are in Him, with a purpose, and a plan. The enemy that lurks is more aware of this truth than most human beings are, and he wants nothing more than to cause each of us to let go of who we are in Christ so we will embrace who the world says we should be. The enemy wants to plant seeds that cause us to doubt the Word of God. At no other time in the history of the world has there been this type of battle waged against the women of God. If we were to believe the world at large, women are worth so much less now than we ever have been before. That's saying a lot considering there are cultures that for centuries have seen women as less valuable than a dog or a rat. The darkness in this world is trying to make us believe that who we were born to be as women of God is not real or valuable. On top of that, we are being told that men can become us and we can choose to vacate who we were born to be, as if God's plan for our lives was an al a carte menu that we can pick and choose from, tossing out whatever we don't like in His plan.

The great news is that God has called each woman of God to be ready for this fight and has equipped us for it. He hasn't left us high and dry. He has given us weapons that we must embrace and use in this fight. For the fight is not just against what we can see through social media, entertainment and politics. The fight is against the ruler of darkness that is working hard to create confusion and distractions in the Body of Christ. Look around and you will see that church after church has mistaken the outpouring of love we're supposed to show all people, no matter their background, their sins, their perceived sins and confusion, with accepting and embracing the sin. Various churches and denominations have declared that they stand with the darkness rather than shining a light on the truth of who we women of God were born to be.

STANDING FIRM

What can each of us to do to be prepared for this battle, to know who we are, to embrace it, to stand our ground and not be moved?

Ephesians 6:11 says, "[11] Put on the full armor of God, so that you can take your stand against the devil's schemes. This word from Paul to the Ephesians tells us that we are called to stand firm against the schemes of the devil. We are given a full set of armor that isn't just available to us for a short time. It's here for us every day. It doesn't just make for a great poster on the wall in the youth room at church. It's real. It's applicable and here for us to put on."

One of my favorite quotes about the armor of God comes from Stormie Omartian. "Ephesians

6:13 is not a suggestion. It is a commandment. We are told to take action. The Bible would not have told us to take up the full armor of God in order to withstand evil if evil could have been withstood without doing so."

I did a series on the armor of God on my Woman Inspired Podcast. It still is one of the most listened to and downloaded series I've done so far. I believe that's telling. Women all over the world are feeling attacked. Many of us sense and discern that who God made us to be has become an affront to those who are of the world and we must be prepared to battle the darkness that threatens to overtake us and dismantle our identity.

One thing stressed in my podcast was that while we were given the armor of God, He won't force us to use it. I ask though, what would happen to a solider out in the desert or in a jungle if he or she didn't put on their camouflage clothing, their helmets and their gun? And if a police officer didn't armor up with a bullet proof vest? They'd be walking out into the battle unarmed with nothing to protect their body, their brain or their limbs.

Ephesians 6: 10 - 17 gives us the information we need to help protect ourselves and to stand firm in this fight for our identity. "[10] Finally, be strong in the Lord and in his mighty power. [11] Put on the full armor of God, so that you can take your stand against the devil's schemes. [12] For our struggle is not against flesh and blood, but against the rulers, against the authorities, against the powers of this dark world and against the spiritual forces of evil in the heavenly realms. [13] Therefore put on the full armor of God, so that when the day of evil comes, you may be able to stand your ground, and after you have done everything, to stand. [14] Stand firm then, with the belt of truth buckled around your waist, with the breastplate of righteousness in place, [15] and with your feet fitted with the readiness that comes from the gospel of peace. [16] In addition to all this, take up the shield of faith, with which you can extinguish all the flaming arrows of the evil one. [17] Take the helmet of salvation and the sword of the Spirit, which is the word of God."

Take note here in verse 13 and 14 where it says, "[13] Therefore put on the full armor of God, so that when the day of evil comes, you may be able to stand your ground, and after you have done everything, to stand. [14] Stand firm then..." It specifically says we have to PUT ON the full armor of God. We're not being forced to. We have a choice.

It also says WHEN the day of evil comes, not IF the day of evil comes. My sisters in Christ, women of God, today is that day. Evil has come. We must armor ourselves up against the evil forces and STAND FIRM…by putting on the full armor of God.

Like it or not, we are in a spiritual battle every single day of our lives and the closer it comes to the return of the Lord, the greater the battle will be. Why? Because the world has evil in it and evil would love nothing more than to stop every single one of us in our tracks and keep us from doing God's will. Evil wants us to give up, give in, lie down and say yes to the world's ever changing standards of who it says we are. Evil wants us to get drunk, cheat on our spouses, become addicted to social media, put our careers first, abandon or abort our children, become full of ourselves, take our loved ones for granted, and stress us out to the point we have to take medication every single day just to handle the smallest amount of anxiety. So, why do we go out without being armored up? We wonder why we end up afraid, stressed, in a lump on the bed in the middle of the day or in the wee hours of the morning, pleading for God to help us when all the while He has, He was, He still is and He has given us armor to help protect us. But we have to choose to put that armor on and be prepared daily for the battle ahead of us.

Philippians 1:27 says, "27 Whatever happens, conduct yourselves in a manner worthy of the gospel of Christ. Then, whether I come and see you or only hear about you in my absence, I will know that you stand firm in the one Spirit, striving together as one for the faith of the gospel…"

Paul has written to the Philippians in this scripture, reminding them to conduct themselves in a manner that is worthy of the gospel of Christ. In doing so, he is reassuring them that even if he isn't watching over their shoulder to make sure they're doing the right thing, he has confidence that they will stand firm in one Spirit. That is the same call to action each of us today has been given - to stand firm. We have been given the commission to be on the ready and be prepared.

KAREN MCCRACKEN

PUTTING ON THE ARMOR OF GOD TO USE IN THE BATTLE FOR YOUR IDENTITY

The belt of truth

Ephesians 6:14 says, "[14]Stand firm then, with the belt of truth buckled around your waist..."

Lies are destructive. Even a supposed little white lie can become destructive. Having been what some people might call naive, especially when I was younger and sadly for many years of my life, I was hurt over and over again by other people's lies. It made me desire truth all the more though. Even if you're truthful about everything, it does not mean you're perfect. None of us is perfect. We have all sadly lied about something in our lives, but the quest to be truthful and seek truth should ever be part of our daily walk. Just as importantly, sharing the truth should be part of our walk. As we all know, no one is perfect except Jesus but that does not mean that we should believe the lies that Satan says about us.

The belt of truth refers to Jesus Christ. When we're told to put on the belt of truth, it means to clothe ourselves with Jesus Christ. Pastor Colin Smith from, OpentheBible.com puts it like this: "The truth is IN Jesus. Truth flows from Jesus, the King of the universe, and God himself. As the second person of the trinity, He created all things, so any truth finds its roots, its source, in Jesus Christ."

We've heard around us in media, on social media, in books and memes for well over a decade now, that we're supposed to listen to, pay attention to and respect someone else's truth. These statements blatantly leave out any mention of the source and creator of truth, Jesus Christ. If everyone is supposedly walking in some other 'truth' than Jesus Christ, then how does that work and what in the world does that mean? How can you have a 'truth' and I have a 'truth', yet they are complete different versions? Social media has a 'truth'. Satan has a 'truth'. Yet, none of these 'truths' match up with each other or with the Word of God. That means none of these supposed various truths are one hundred percent true. So, what in the world is the truth about the truth? What I found out is that there is but one truth; THE truth. There is just plain truth that stems from Jesus Christ; not my truth, not your truth, not her truth, nor his truth, but one truth and that is THE truth given to us by the Word of God and the presence of Jesus Christ. This is what we are to clothe ourselves with.

I actually think one of the biggest lies and manipulations evil has set in motion in the last decade or two is convincing people that there are multiple truths about one thing rather than just the truth. You do have your own experiences, and you have your own feelings about the truth. You have your own memories as well as your own opinions. But that doesn't change the truth, which usually typically lies somewhere outside of our own fallible, easily deceived human brains. Right? For some people, it's not about fallibility; it's about them wanting to lie. It's about them feeling some desire or need to lie for attention, affection, pride and vanity. It's about a person being drawn into a pattern of evil thinking and sinful choices.

Our job as children of God is to take every bit of info, whatever we think and feel, whatever we are shown, whatever we listen to, whatever we read, whatever we study, whatever we experience or share and make sure that we put it through the filter of discernment that we've been blessed with so that we can know if it's true or not. In doing so, our discernment must also make sure that whatever we believe matches up with God's Word.

If you look around the world today and think, "There is no truth anymore. There is not one who can be trusted." You are not alone. But it is not impossible to find the truth. In fact, we are called to be pursuers of truth as well as people who share the truth. Please remember on the days you get discouraged, that God's not going to ask us to do something that He doesn't equip us to do.

1 Thessalonians 5:16-22 says, "[16] Always be joyful. [17] Never stop praying. [18] Be thankful in all circumstances, for this is God's will for you who belong to Christ Jesus. [19] Do not stifle the Holy Spirit. [20] Do not scoff at prophecies, [21] but test everything that is said. Hold on to what is good. [22] Stay away from every kind of evil."

Now, all of that may seem difficult but it states right here in **1 Thessalonians 5:16-22** that this is God's will for us. Don't stifle the Holy Spirit. Allow Him to give you information and discernment but don't scoff at prophecy. But test everything according to the truth. Test everything that is said and hold on to good. Test it, research it and ask questions. Don't believe blindly. There are many untruths being thrown out in this world today by everyday people in everyday situations that we have to be diligent to seek out the truth and use the truth to protect ourselves.

Truth is an absolute, it is not flexible. In other words, if the truth is that you are a human being, then you're a human being and that's not changing. You can't change yourself into a fluffy panda bear. That won't happen. Now, you can dress up like a fluffy panda bear. You can wear a cute costume and sit in a bamboo tree for a month, but it won't change you into a real panda bear. You are a woman and you were called to walk as a woman of God. You can try to run from the truth but it is absolute truth and no matter how far from the truth you go, it will still always be the truth. Lies of the world and those derived from devilish confusion would have you believing otherwise.

Truth is also defined, "as a body of real things, facts or events" (Miriam Webster). Truth is also a spiritual or fundamental reality. This is what much of today's world comes down to anymore is what is real vs. what is fake. Just have a peek around technology and you will see a large array of fake everything. There are so many lies. Even going into a grocery store assaults us with fakery. We're surrounded by small lies that we have gradually fully accepted as truth even in our everyday shopping. Think about it. We would consider them in society as a marketing ploy or 'little white lies'. But if you pick up a carton of generic strawberry ice cream, it says strawberry on it, though it's likely not. You have to be diligent. You have to discern. You have to research. You have to open your eyes and read in the tiny, tiny print where it says "strawberry flavored".

The belt of truth is something we're given to help us understand what is truth and what is false and yet we willingly believe even the littlest of lies, accepting deception in the smallest areas of our lives, like there being no real strawberries in some strawberry ice cream. Or a product declaring it was new and improved when nothing was changed but the packaging. Yet, we grab, buy it and believe it for a time. In the big lies and what the world calls the little white lies, we must learn to use the belt of truth to protect ourselves. The scripture says stand firm then with the belt of truth buckled around your waist. How can the truth be something you buckle around your waist? Is it even possible? Do they have a barcode scanner for that? Can we just scan a product, a person, a family member or a politician to see if it beeps and alerts us to their lies? That would be far easier than sharpening our discernment and taking the time to pray, research and test whether or not something is the truth. It's just not how it works.

Why do you think God equated truth with a belt? Let's think about the design of a belt. It's wrapped around the middle of our body, sometimes a bit higher or lower depending on your style and your body shape. But pretty much it hits right at the core of your body. (Truth also hits us there too – right at the center of who we are and at the center of everything.) A belt is something that is worn closest to us. The truth is something that we should also hold close to us and keep at the core or the center of everything. It's fitting that the belt of truth is listed as the first piece of armor in the armor of God because Jesus is the way, <u>the truth,</u> and the life and no one goes to The Father except through Him. (**John 14:16**) So therefore, truth is on the top of the list of importance in the daily walk of a Christian. Without truth the rest of the armor would be of no use to us whatsoever because we would not be able to see the truth or value in what the rest of the armor does for us. We wouldn't even know the truth of the fact that we actually need armor.

If we didn't have truth, we wouldn't be able to trust the discernment given to us or be able to identify falsehoods that get thrown at us every single day. Without truth we wouldn't be able to discern how or when God is calling us to move, or to stay, to go, or take a leap of faith or to be still. Without truth, we wouldn't be able to learn or embrace the rest of the gospel or understand the hope for which we live because without truth, we wouldn't be able to accept or process or pay attention to prophecy or to revelation or to the prompting of the Holy Spirit without having the truth wrapped around the very core of our being. We certainly wouldn't be able to discern good from evil without THE truth.

It says in the Bible that in the last days they will call what is good, evil and what is evil, good. "They" being those who do not know what the truth is - those who haven't armored up. It's speaking of those who have been deceived and refused to put on the belt of truth. They will be duped. They will be successfully attacked, manipulated, deceived and destroyed in the name of good and in the name of something that calls itself good. When in all actuality, it is evil.

Let's think about it even a little more logically. If you're in need of armor, then you're in a battle or you're getting ready to be. God knew we would be under attack for belonging to Him so He graciously equipped us for this battle between truth and lies. When you dissect the belt that belongs with a suit of armor, you need to know that the belt isn't just there holding up a warrior's pants! No, it also has a place on it to hold one of the most important pieces of the armor, the sword of the Spirit. The belt on a warrior also holds small tools like food and other things to help sustain a warrior in battle. But most importantly, it helps gird the person wearing it. What do I mean by that? The word gird means to "prepare oneself for action or to make something secure," (Miriam Webster) such as securing the sword to the body of a warrior. God obviously knew that we would need to be girded; secure in knowing the truth. He knew we would need the armor He gave us in order to help us in our battles. As we each make our way on this journey He set before us, we will need that armor. He knew that little lies, big lies from people and all of evil's lies would set us up for personal attacks that threaten to weaken us. But He knew what we were heading for, and praise Him, He gave us spiritual armor.

I encourage you to sit quietly and have the Holy Spirit show you the times when you didn't put that belt of truth on and how it would have or could have changed your life in those instances had you been wearing it. If you had, how would it have changed your relationships and your walk with God? Because even though you can't change the past, you can learn from it. So, if you think about it, if you had known the truth in certain situations; the truth of who other people were, the truth of who you are; the truth of who the Lord is, how would it have changed your walk up to this point?

I can look back and see times how I was affected before I even knew about the belt of truth and times I knew but just didn't pick it up because I was spiritually lazy and didn't want to make the effort. We're human like that, aren't we? Sometimes we just prefer to be deceived because frankly, it comforts us in our sin to know we aren't alone. Sometimes we prefer sin to obedience. Unfortunately, there are always natural consequences to when we sin and then we will have to answer for it when we see Him face to face. But in the moment, it's easy to embrace a lie and go with it – until we get hurt, that is.

There have been times I didn't see truth from lies because I didn't wrap myself in truth. I didn't allow it to be at the core of who I was. I chose not to be girded with the truth. Doing so makes it easier to lie to yourself and to other people and it makes it easier to accept lies and somehow justify sinful actions. Not be girded also allows us to be deceived in a mighty way by Satan and by the temptations of this world. Perhaps you're in a place right now where you haven't put on the belt of truth ever in your life because you're afraid that in doing so you will see a truth you're not prepared to see. Or perhaps your own lies will be exposed. Woman of God, do not fear. If you are afraid, take heart because we have a Savior who is a forgiver of all who come to Him and pour themselves out. He is not here to condemn you and in fact, He is waiting for each of us to not only stop deceiving others and ourselves but waiting for us to stand up, stand firm and stop letting Satan deceive us, calling us evil when all along He said that what He made was good. (Genesis 1:31)

Using the belt of truth in the battle for your identity:

Are you unsure if you're walking around with the belt of truth on or not? If you've said any of the following recently, the likelihood is you've left the belt off and your pants are dropping. Pray, hold on...you may about to be exposed.

I already turned that paper in. (Yet you forgot to do turn it in.)

Not sure why you didn't receive it yet. (Knowing all the while you forgot to send it.)

I left the house 10 minutes ago. (Even though you have yet to get dressed.)

Sure, I can do that for you. (Though you have no intention of following through.)

You look great. Have you lost weight? (As you say to yourself, "She looks rough.")

I can't come in today, I have a migraine. (As you pack to go to the lake for the day.)

OR perhaps you aren't wearing that belt of truth and the consequence is you believe any or all of the following:

You're not good enough.

You might as well give up.

It's ok to lie this time.

Don't worry about cheating. Everyone does it.

You'll never be good enough unless you have more money.

You can only move ahead if you go drinking with the boss.

Don't worry; no one will know you stole that.

The Bible is outdated.

Revelation is just fairy tales

You have nothing in life to live for.

You will never be loved or accepted.

You were a mistake.

And the biggest lies that come at us are that Jesus didn't die for us. Jesus doesn't love us. Jesus could never forgive us for what we've done.

But if we know what the truth is, if we start by putting on the belt of truth so we're protected, then we'll know what the lies are when we encounter them. If we clothe ourselves with Jesus Christ, being in Him and the truth of who He is, we have then begun to put on the armor of God to protect ourselves. Not only does it bring us discernment about who we are but it protects us from the lies of the enemy and the world.

Woman of God, stand firm:

- Make 2 lists for yourself; for your eyes and God's purposes only. List 1 is a list of lies you know you've said that you have not repented of or taken to the Lord and asked forgiveness for. Pour them out. Ask God to shine the light on where you've sinned so you can come to Him and confess, repent and turn your back on those lies, with the determination that you will pick up the belt of truth and work from here forward to be truthful in all ways.

- List 2 will be a list of lies you've been told that you have believed; specifically lies about who you are and who you aren't. Ask for God's direction and discernment in this process. It's not an easy one. Sometimes we have believed something about ourselves for so long that we are convinced of its truth. But picking up the belt of truth will help you. Clothing yourself with Christ in this way will show you the truth. Literally envision yourself picking up the belt of truth as a piece of armor you're ready to gird yourself with and then pray.

You don't have to rush this process. It can take some time. But do it with all your heart and soul. Allow the Holy Spirit to move you and show you.

Sometimes it can take stepping back for a bit to pray about each lie and ask for the Lord to illuminate it for you. Sometimes it can take allowing someone else to join you in the process. Choose someone you know will be honest with you but with whom you feel safe sharing. Allow them to pray with you and help you confront the lies.

Once you have done all these things then you can use the belt of truth for another purpose that it was intended for – to share the truth of the gospel of Jesus Christ. Once you have confronted the lies you've been told about who you are in the Lord and you know who you are, you can walk confidently in the truth of His love, grace and mercy, sharing it with others.

The breast plate of righteousness

Ephesians 6:14 says, "¹⁴Stand firm then...with the breastplate of righteousness in place,"

How will righteousness protect us and can we just put on righteousness like it's a piece of clothing? Really, is it that easy? No, it's not always easy but it's worth the effort to put righteousness in the place it belongs, freely accepting what God has offered us through it. If we do not protect ourselves with righteousness, we open ourselves up to attack from the enemy that can be spiritually fatal to our journey. What I want more than anything on this path of purpose is to be obedient and to accept every good thing God has for me. Righteousness means to be right in God's eyes or; "to live right, to have right thinking and make right choices" (Miriam Webster) The kicker is, that means RIGHT according to what God says is right, not of our own sinful-leaning, or of our own weary minds, skewed thinking and most definitely not what the world says is right. What is right or righteous to the world is ever-changing. From one season to the next, the definition of what is righteous can change in the eyes of current culture. To be righteous means to obey God's commandments and live in a way that is honorable to Him.

When you hear about the breastplate of righteousness, do you think about it protecting your heart, and vital organs like an actual roman soldier's breastplate did? I think the imagery here is super important because it shows us that in righteousness there is protection from fatal spiritual blows. If we live outside the Lord it could truly be eternally fatal. A spiritual death is far worse than a physical one. This righteousness, God's holiness and perfection, comes to us through Jesus' death and resurrection on the cross. That is NOT something we should take lightly.

Crosswalk.com says "Righteousness doesn't mean saying a prayer once and then going on with our lives as though nothing has changed. Justification comes through a one-time commitment to Christ. Sanctification, the act of God shaping us to become more like Him, happens over a lifetime." That's where righteous living comes in to play.

So, in order to live honorably and in a way that

God wants us to, we have to know HOW He wants us to live. We have to read the Bible, commit to studying His Word, and choose to be in prayer and relationship with Him. We have to know what the truth of His Word is, measuring everything according to what the Word says, not what the world says.

So, what does God say is right living? Right now you can Google a question or a topic and find loads of commentary on just about anything, but how do you know which piece of information is true? Many churches today have different versions of what they say the truth is, how we should or shouldn't live and what they say God condones or doesn't condone. But let me share something with you: we also have been given THE truth in the Word of God and as I already outlined, as part of our spiritual armor, we have been given that belt of truth. Here's the interesting thing; when a soldier put on his armor, he first had to put on the belt before he could put on the breastplate we're talking about. Why? Because the armor was heavy. A set of armor weighed around 70 pounds. Much of that weight was in the breastplate itself. In order for the breastplate to be held up and to stay in place, it had to rest on the belt. The belt literally helped hold up the breastplate. The breastplate would be considered the most important part of a soldier's armor because one blow to the chest or arrow or bullet to the chest and the soldier could fall or die. But the breastplate could not be worn without first wearing the belt that helped hold it up.

Spiritually speaking, about this amazing armor God gave us, the breastplate of righteousness cannot be utilized without it resting on the belt of truth. You cannot know the fullness of righteousness and right living or right thinking in the Lord without first knowing the truth. Righteousness rests on the truth. The truth is not merely something dished up in a Sunday service or even in a Christian podcast like the one I do weekly. Yes, I share Biblical truths and I pray over everything I share and say, as do most speakers, teachers and preachers, but seeking and knowing the truth is also a personal responsibility. It's an action we have to do as individuals, as children of God. We aren't given this spiritual armor when we're born, when we get involved in a church but because we have entered the family of God through freely accepting Jesus Christ as our Lord and Savior and believing. We are given this armor as a gift, as protection, as something we're told is vital to our spiritual living and to our protection when we become believers by accepting the Lord, and loving Him. Again, we then have to choose to pick it up though. WE have to pick it up. God is not going to thrust it upon us or force us to use it. So, first you have to pick up and put on the truth, and then you can clothe yourself with righteousness.

I ask you, what's getting in the way of you living the way God wants you to? Is there something or someone who is derailing your efforts to clothe yourself with the breastplate of righteousness? Is it your past? Your present? Fear of your future? Are you supported by a church, a denomination, a Bible study group that encourages you to seek the truth? Are you prayed for as you work to pick up that belt of truth and hoist up that righteous living? Or are you hanging out with the same old friends, doing that same old same old thing you know you shouldn't be doing? Are you stuck in old unrighteous thoughts and actions, all the while crying out to God, asking why He hasn't protected you, why He lets you get into difficult situations and hurt? And yet, you aren't even using the armor He gave you?

If you answered yes to any of those questions, then you're walking around spiritually naked. Perhaps you've even decided to use other things to attempt to protect yourself. Have you been putting blinders on to what's going on in the world, even though you've been given the opportunity to sharpen your discernment and walk in truth? Are you just going with the flow, too busy, too tired, too enamored with culture's worldly ideas of what is good and right to dare make time to step into a church or pick up your Bible? Are you going with the flow of the world, no matter where the flow takes you and without seeking if your choices are flowing with the truth?

Maybe, just maybe, you're one of those people who has lived a certain way, with certain traditions and beliefs most of your life but not because you sought out the truth but because it was easier to keep your head in the sand, blinders on and let other peoples words and religious traditions supposedly protect you. Or maybe you fear something outside of what you've always done and always known, or you fear rejection from the very people, family and friends who are intentionally or unintentionally keeping you from the truth of God's Word? Do you fear rejection from others more than you fear God? More than you love God? Then if so, I can say with sincerity, I doubt you're wearing the armor of God and that sadly means you are not protected like you could be or should be.

Here's the thing, women of God, in order to truly live a righteous life, we have to live as the Lord says. We have to be determined to do as God's Word says, not doing what religious dogma and man-made traditions dictate. We cannot live in fear of rejection, letting that fear make our choices for us. We cannot define who we are according to what the traditions of our family have been or according to who our relatives say we are. If you are being defined as a person of a certain status, denomination, tradition, or nature that is contrary to the righteous living God says you should be defined by, then you must pick up your breastplate of righteousness and battle for your true identity. It is up to each of us to seek out the truth of who the Lord is and what the Word of God actually says about who we are and how we are to live according to His definition of righteousness.

Using the breastplate of righteousness in the battle for your identity

Women of God, each of us has to read the Word for ourselves to know how to live. The truth of who Jesus Christ is, how we should live and who we are is plainly given to us in the Word. When we have His truth solidly wrapped around us, THEN we can pick up that breastplate of righteousness that causes us not just to want to live a righteous, Godly life, but to learn how to live a righteous Godly life and define ourselves accordingly. This kind of living helps protect us from foes, from foolishness, from lies and attacks, as it illuminates our paths so if we stumble and fall we will be protected.

Are you wondering if God can actually protect you with a breastplate of righteousness? Are you concerned that righteous living is something you can ever achieve? I've had those doubts in my life too. Like many other women of God, I've been hurt and I've hurt others. For many years, because of that hurt, I thought God didn't care. I thought there was no longer any protection for me. I also defined myself as a victim and someone who needs forgiveness but cannot be forgiven. I became unforgivable in my own mind. I believed the lies that Satan and other people were telling me. I was not worthy of forgiveness. I even got to the point I was one step away from saying, "Fine, if I'm not forgivable, I will live like there's no such thing as forgiveness and do whatever I want."

My heart was hurting, my spirit ached. Through studying the Word and immersing myself in prayer, I learned that God was not the enemy. I was an enemy to myself at times and the creator of my own pitfalls. I learned that we all have free will and sadly we are able to take that free will to purposefully hurt others. But through Jesus there is hope. Through His truth there is freedom. Through His forgiveness there is a grace and mercy waiting for each of us; all of us. This is why I choose to take up the armor of God now, refusing to let myself be defined as a constant victim or as someone who is weak and living a life without truth or righteousness. While I am not perfect, I am blessed to be offered the gift of clothing myself with the truth of Jesus Christ and working to pick up the righteous way of living He offers me every single day. When I do these things, I can battle what the world says about who I am. When I choose armoring up, He prepares for me a place of refuge in Him during this battle against my identity and against an enemy who wants me to believe that I am neither forgiven, nor worthy of love.

I have chosen to stand firm, taking up the full armor of God, beginning with the belt of truth and the breastplate of righteousness. I encourage you to do the same. **Proverbs 30:5** says, "5 Every word of God is flawless; he is a shield to those who take refuge in him." Are you needing refuge and respite to pray, and meditate on the Word? To talk to God and let Him lead you?

Woman of God, stand firm:

- If you don't have a dedicated place to pray, make one. Whether it's in the corner of the spare room, in a chair near your bed, or on the floor in the closet. Make a dedicated space for yourself. In this space, make the time every single day to open your heart to Jesus. Pour out to Him where you've stubbornly refused to embrace righteous living and seek His direction daily to make each day an opportunity to take up that breastplate and try again.

- As you pray, ask the Lord to open your eyes to see how you've been defining yourself and whether or not that definition matches up to who He says you are. Ask Him to correct your thinking, clear your vision and then allow Him to be your refuge and hiding place when the truth of who you thought you were is replaced by who He says you actually are. There is freedom in knowing the truth but it can be painful to let go of old ideas, thoughts and patterns. When we're hurt we become more vulnerable to attacks from the enemy, so plan to take refuge in the strength and love of the Lord. Sit in His presence as you take in the truths He shows you in your dedicated quiet time each day.

- Consciously envision yourself taking up the breastplate of righteousness and putting it on. Know that this shield you carry will help protect your heart in Christ Jesus and walk accordingly throughout your day.

The shoes of the gospel of peace

Ephesians 6:15 says, "[15] and with your feet fitted with the readiness that comes from the gospel of peace."

The shoes of the gospel of peace mean that we have been given the charge that no matter where we walk, we share the gospel with others. We're supposed to be prepared, always having the gospel in our hearts with us wherever we go, so we can share it with others. It's our duty to share God's love. First we have to immerse ourselves in it, to know it, and then we'll be able to go out in the world to share the gospel with others. In peace, we are to show others the love of Christ, pray for them, pray with them, and be prepared or "fitted with readiness" on every road our journey leads us down.

This verse in Ephesians is phrased a bit differently in various Bible translations but each one gives us a good perspective and reminder of just what it is we're charged with while we wear this armor.

The New Living Translation (NLT) says in **Ephesians 6:15**: "For shoes, put on the peace that comes from the Good news so that you will be fully prepared."

Now, in case you didn't know, when it refers to the gospel of peace in these verses, it means the message that Jesus gave to those who trust Him. It's the message of assurance that those who believe and love the Lord are in His hands; that He's got us; that He is our Messiah and our Savior. The word readiness, which is used in the New International Version (NIV) translation, according to the dictionary means "constant vigilance". A soldier in battle has to be vigilant, consistent, at the ready to battle against the enemy's tactics and tricks. Being ready means you know who your enemy is and what he will likely do next. The NIV translation says, "…and with your feet fitted with the readiness that comes from the gospel of peace."

A soldier has to be ready at all times. His shoes back in the days when armor was worn were studded with nails or spikes and they had cleats on the bottom, or little spikes like soccer and football players or some track and field athletes wear to give them traction and assist them to stay upright and stable on uneven ground. They also helped them stay balanced and allowed them to dig in to the ground for traction when needed. No matter how great all a soldier's armor is, if he falls, he has to be able to get back up. The cleats or spikes of the soldier's shoes helped a solider to get his grip and stand upright again when he fell.

In The Message translation of the Bible, which I don't often use yet find very interesting, it states things a bit differently. It's written in a very casual, direct language. Sometimes it leaves out the specific nuances and details that are extremely important in scripture and doesn't always take into consideration the Hebrew or Aramaic root words or original languages, in my opinion. But this particular translation does at times drive the point home in a way that resonates with me. I share it for that reason. It says this: "Be prepared. You're up against far more than you can handle on your own. Take all the help you can get, every weapon God has issued, so that when it's all over but the shouting you'll still be on your feet. Truth, righteousness, peace, faith, and salvation are more than words. Learn how to apply them. You'd need them throughout your life."

These shoes are the shoes OF the gospel of peace. The gospel. Meaning the first 4 books in the New Testament, which are Matthew, Mark, Luke, and John. They contain gospel truth. Not your truth or my truth but THE truth of who Jesus Christ is. The truth of acceptance, repentance, forgiveness, grace, mercy, eternal life, and how we have been blessed with all that through the birth, death, resurrection, ascension and return of our Savior, who will come again. That is the gospel. With knowing the gospel, the true gospel, comes a peace like no other. We are not just protected by this gospel knowledge and truth. We are also charged here with putting the shoes on our feet to walk this walk and share that gospel. We have gospel shoes so that we may walk out our faith. We have shoes on our feet to protect us on the way as we share with others the love of Jesus Christ and the gospel message.

Using the shoes of the gospel of peace in the battle for your identity:

The shoes of the gospel of peace help us in being grounded in the truth, knowledge and peace of the gospel message; allowing us to face an enemy who wants us to fall and to fail. As you walk out your faith, the enemy wants to trip you up, cause you to lose your peace and then stop you in your tracks so you won't share the gospel of peace with others. But we each were given shoes that help ready us. We have the clear gospel message to help combat any lies that are thrown at us about who we are.

When you've had a day of feeling like nothing you've done has succeeded and you feel like a failure, you can use the peace of the gospel to take a deep breath and remember who you actually are. When you slip up, you fall, you choose outside what you know the will of God was for you in the moment, you are fitted with the readiness to be able to turn and pivot, even in an instant. Remember, Women of God, those gospel shoes are likened to the shoes a soldier wears in battle. You will be spiritually ready to stand firm even in the slippery slime of sin that we all sometimes entangle ourselves in. You will not be moved if you stand on the truth of the gospel of peace and refuse to let the enemy pull you down. Use those spiritual spikes to dig in, hold your ground and then move forward, embracing the gospel for yourself and then sharing it with others.

Woman of God, stand firm:

- Each morning as you dress, remind yourself before you head out the door or set forth in your house, that "today I am wearing the shoes of the gospel of peace" and ask the Lord to help make you ready to share that gospel with others. Sometimes we have to look for opportunities to share the love of Christ but more often than not, the opportunities are right in front of us but we get too busy with daily life to even notice them. Pray for your eyes to be opened each and every morning as you go about your day. Pray for the Lord to open your eyes to the blessing of sharing the gospel with others.

- Where you feel ill-prepared, seek guidance on how to become prepared. There is likely not one day that goes by that something or someone is tempting you to accept a version of yourself that's false, that's not who God made you to be. Through TV, movies, social media, and radio we're told we must be this or that and most of it is contrary to what the Word of God tells us. Seek God for the reminders to stay armored up, to walk peacefully on by those who tempt you to fall for the lies of the enemy and pray for the discernment to know what is of Him and what is not.

- Pray daily for the shoes of the gospel of peace to ready you for in battle for your identity. Pray for the shoes to do their job; to steady you, to ready you and allow you to stand firm with the knowledge of who you are according to the gospel.

The shield of faith

Ephesians 6:16 says, "¹⁶ In addition to all this, take up the shield of faith, with which you can extinguish all the flaming arrows of the evil one."

What is faith? Faith, according to **Hebrews 11:1**, "…is confidence in what we hope for and assurance about what we do not see."

The definition of assurance is, "being certain in the mind, lacking doubt; assured." (Miriam Webster) If we are certain in our minds and without doubt about who the Lord Jesus Christ is and of the truth of the Word of God then we are walking in faith. But how does having confidence in what we hope for and lack of doubt protect us?

Since Paul shares in Ephesians that faith is a shield in the armor of God, let's look at it by first describing what a shield does to protect a soldier. According to biblestudy.org, a shield was great protection and the first line of defense for a Roman soldier. "Because of its sheer size, about three and a half feet tall and almost three feet wide; soldiers were afforded a great deal of protection from enemies. Because of its slight curve, it was able to deflect attacks without transferring the full force of the assault to the man holding the shield...it was able to deflect even the more vicious blows and function in a limited offensive capacity as a means of knocking an opponent backwards".

For a Roman soldier, the shield would be used to deflect arrows, flaming arrows, stones and objects being propelled at them. Remember, the scripture says, "...take up the shield of faith, with which you can extinguish all the flaming arrows of the evil one. " The imagery here is clearly showing that Satan will shoot fiery arrows or darts of doubt, temptation, manipulation, lies, distraction, fear, anxiety, confusion, family destruction, and even more, directly at the children of God and even every human being who has yet to come into the family of God. Make no bones about it though, Women of God, he's shooting specific arrows at us, trying to get a direct hit to his target, causing us to doubt who we are in Christ, confuse us and destroy our true identity.

The shield of a Roman soldier would cover much of the core body, offering him greater chance of survival in a direct attack. It wasn't some small round Captain America comic book style shield. The massive shield could be used by soldiers in direct hand-to-hand combat, soldier upon soldier, not just to shield the soldier but also as a weapon itself. You can well imagine how heavy a shield would be that is large enough to cover most men from knee caps up to the chest area. When a soldier was strong enough to wield the shield as a weapon, you can imagine that it was well able to knock down an enemy.

The many shields in a great army also helped protect more than just one soldier at a time. Have you ever seen movies where the soldiers lined up, bearing their shields, standing shoulder to shoulder? They did this in a move to create a barrier or a wall of shields in order to keep the enemy from entering the gates of their kingdom.

Now imagine faith as your shield, as Ephesians tells us. Faith, being held up against the world can deflect the fiery arrows of the enemy as he shoots lies, deception, manipulation and temptation at us. If we use our faith to block the attacks of the enemy, walking in the truth we know through the Word of God, we have far less need to use the other armor God has supplied us with because we have blocked the attack. Greater still, if we as the Body of Christ were to stand should to shoulder with our brothers and sisters in Christ, raising our faith up as a shield against the enemy and attacks of the world, we would be able to stand strong against the enemy who seeks to kill and destroy the church.

The enemy knows that faith in God and consistent showing of that faith is a sign he's wasting his time. The Bible says in **James 4: 7**, "Submit yourselves then, to God. Resist the devil, and he will flee from you." Satan knows what faith looks like. When we resist Satan and allow our faith to be put first and foremost in front of who we are, in front of our own desires, our own doubts and fears, then we are showing the enemy that we will resist him and submit only to God. He will then flee.

The shield of faith is the only piece of armor Paul shares about in Ephesians 6 that we don't actually wear. We have to pick it up. We don't put it on. We have to hold it up. Every piece of the armor is offered to us but not forced on us. The same goes for the shield of faith. It says we must "take up" the shield of faith.

If you have faith in God, then you have faith in His Word and the knowledge that it is true. The Bible says, "Thy Word is a lamp unto my feet and a light unto my path." (**Psalm 119:105**). So much of the Word of God illuminates who He is to us and who we are in Him. If you have faith, then you will embrace the scriptures that bring light and truth to your path and to every situation you will encounter, in turn protecting you as you hold on to faith like a shield, knowing that you are protected from the lies of the enemy.

Using the shield of faith in the battle for your identity:

Do you have faith that God will do what He says He will do? Do you have faith, without seeing Him face to face in this moment, that the Lord is with you all of your days and that He will fulfill His promises? If you do, then the protection you have through that faith is as great as the protection a Roman soldier got from his shield in battle.

When my faith was small and I was going through a painful divorce, I believed the lies the enemy told me. I believed that no one would ever want me again. I believed that I wasn't good enough to be with a Godly man so I submitted myself to an ungodly man. Had I been strong in my faith, picking up the shield to block the fiery darts of lies and temptation shot at me by the enemy, I would have stayed grounded and stood firm on the truth of who I was in Christ Jesus. In doing so, I would never have strayed or allowed myself to become involved with someone who totally and completely lived outside the gospel. Praise God, as I fell, He caught me. He raised me up and set my feet back on solid ground, allowing me to repent, turn away from my disobedience and be reminded of who I was in Him. He will do the same for you, no matter how small your faith may seem in this moment, and no matter how far away from Him you think you are. He is still here for you, ready and willing to welcome you back and longing for you to pick your armor back up. You need not doubt that He loves you and that what He says He will do in the gospel message, He will do.

When your faith is big and strong, it will stand up against any fiery message of lies that Satan will shoot at you. When you're told you can't be forgiven, you will know that's not true. When you are tempted to be unfaithful to prove to your spouse that someone still wants you, you will say no to that temptation because you have faith that God loves you and wants you, even if your spouse leaves you. With the Lord, you will never be alone. When your faith is strong, the truth of who you are in the Lord is protected behind a mighty shield. The Woman of God that you are may be called in to question by a world that believes a Godly woman is a woman with little or no value but through your faith, you can believe that God made you to be who you are, at just the right time, for just the right purpose, and for just the right plan.

Woman of God, stand firm:

- Embrace faith. As you study the Word of God, see throughout the Bible, most specifically the books of the Major Prophets (Isaiah, Jeremiah, Ezekiel, Daniel, Lamentations and in the book of

Revelation), that what He said He will do, He has done and will continue to do. Understand through studying His actions that His Word is truth. The Lord has nothing to prove to us yet He has proven it. Time and time again, we can see through His Word that He is a God you need not doubt. Take time over the next months to research and study the prophecies that have come true and bolster up your faith through what He has revealed to us in His Word

- As you go about your day, go back to the scriptures that correlate to who God says you are and remind yourself that as you take up your shield of faith, this is who you are protecting. You are protecting a Woman of God who is chosen (**1 Thess. 1:4**), strong (**Phil. 4:13**), beautiful (**Eccl. 3:11**), known (**Psalm 139:1**), wonderful (**Psalm 139:14**), victorious (**Romans 8:37**). So when the lies of the world and the enemy try to tell you that you are not these things, you can deflect their lies.

- Though this scripture in Isaiah is reminding the people of Israel who they are and how God protects them, it is also applicable to us today. Let this verse wash over you and remind you who your faith is in and why. "¹Do not fear, for I have re-

Redeemed you, I have summoned you by name; you are mine. [2] When you pass through the waters, I will be with you; and when you pass through the rivers, they will not sweep over you. When you walk through the fire, you will not be burned; the flames will not set you ablaze. [3] For I am the LORD your God, the Holy One of Israel, your Savior;" - **Isaiah 43:1-3**. Pray and ask the Lord to remind you that you are His and He is yours; that He has summoned you, He has called you, and you need not fear

The helmet of salvation

Ephesians 6:17 says, "¹⁷ Take the helmet of salvation and the sword of the Spirit, which is the word of God."

Part of the armor of God Paul talks about is the helmet of salvation. This imagery used to make me giggle to be quite honest, because when I think of a helmet, I think of football. In my mind I used to see 12 disciples in football helmets. But even with that kind of helmet, this imagery makes sense in so many ways. The head is pretty much the most essential part of a person's physical being and in the Bible you can see how the head is considered basically the same as the whole person. In other words, the head represents who the person is. For example, it illustrates this on biblestudytools.org: "People would place their hands on the head of a person when that person was being blessed. Check out Matthew 19:15. They aren't just blessing the head, but the head is prayed over. When curses were made in the Bible, they would fall on someone's head. (Genesis 49:26). And in Genesis 3:15 when Jesus crushes the head of the serpent, it's a blow that can't be come back from." The blow to the head was final, totally destroying the serpent.

Think about this in political terms, and Kingdom terms. When you have a leader of a country, a company, a committee, they're called the head: i.e. heads of state, heads of committees. They are the head over all the body that they represent. As Christians, we are supposed to have a head of the family. You have someone who sits at the head of the table, who usually leads the table in prayer yet represents the entire group of people at the table or in the family. People who are considered the head of something are supposed to help protect and lead the entire body.

So, when I think of this part of the armor of God, I think of head gear, specifically a helmet in this day and age. Not sure about you but I specifically think of a football helmet, bike helmet, or even a motorcycle helmet. Back in Roman times, their helmet design was naturally different. They weren't made for protection during playing games but for going to war and being in battle.

Helmets back then were not made on a manufacturing line. They weren't made from strong plastics or high-tech materials that can withstand loads of pressure and high heat like they are today. They had to be forged individually to fit a soldier's head, which meant that no two helmets were exactly alike. They all had some differences to them even though there was a basic safety design in each era, just as there is today in sports. What NFL players wore for safety 10 and 20 years ago is quite different than what they wear today. Usually, the helmets of Roman soldiers were all metal with fabric or leather padding in some of them. It depended on how much money you had and what your station in life was what kind of helmet you were afforded. People who were considered poor usually had leather helmets that were just fortified with metal pieces rather than all metal helmets because leather was cheaper and easier to get than metal was.

No matter the design, the purpose of the helmet was to protect against deadly blows to the head just like helmets in modern day sports are intended to do. Soldiers in war today still wear helmets that are specifically designed for their station, and purpose, for maximum protection and function.

If you think about helmet designs, they're pretty clever and each piece is purposeful. Back when this scripture was written about the armor of

God, the helmets were said to have cheek plates to guard against blows to the face, with a metal piece in the back to protect against a hit to the back of the neck and head. Over time, they started making a lower piece on the front to help cover the eyes to protect them too. But no matter the design, a helmet protects a soldier against damage and deadly blows to the head. Spiritually speaking, in the armor of God, the helmet of salvation protects the mind against anything that could disorient, confuse, trick, weaken or destroy a Christian. It helps keep us from mental attacks, temptations, strikes against our mindset and mental health and protects us from discouragement and deceit.

Can you think of anything at all that has been created, formed, or crafted that just might be waging war against your mind and mindset? Against your brain? Your perspective? Your confidence? Your very identity? Is there any current modern-day invention, technology and social construct that you know of that may be used as a weapon against the brains and heads of people en mass? I think we all know the answer to that question, don't we? Social media.

It's interesting because apparently in Roman warfare, the helmet and the sword were the last two pieces of armor a soldier would put on. With modern military uniforms, it's same thing. A helmet can get hot so it wouldn't be put on unless serious dangers were in play or when a soldier was headed straight into something that would threaten a blow to the head or when a dangerous attack to the head seemed imminent. So, it went on last. The helmet can definitely help a soldier feel safer in battle. At least that is part of the point of it; part of its job. Helmets are time tested, soldier and athlete approved, aren't they? That's the very brief recollection I have of the history of the helmet in a nutshell. If helmets didn't work to help protect the soldier, armies and sports leagues wouldn't keep pouring money into purchasing them and seeking better, safer designs over the years.

So, what does the helmet of salvation mean for believers then? The battlefield we're on most often takes place in our minds. Satan attacks us with fear, lies, doubts, and tries to get us to believe whatever he's throwing at us in order to distract us and hopefully destroy us. I've heard this saying for years from various sources: "If you don't fill your mind with the Word of God, the enemy will fill it with fear, anxiety, stress, worry and temptation." And it's true. When we fill our mind, our daily thoughts and our memories with the Word of God, we take up room that otherwise is open and ideal for the enemy to invade.

When we put on the helmet of salvation, it literally gives us confidence and safety during attacks. It helps protect our minds. Salvation is a protection that comes only from the Lord. The knowledge of who Jesus Christ is, and that we have a hope that is beyond all other hopes (eternal life, grace, and forgiveness) makes a difference in how we think. It makes a difference in how we face each day, each crisis, each decision, each dilemma, and every attack of the enemy. Knowing that we have eternal life, eternal hope, forgiveness, grace, assistance, love, acceptance and all the amazing gifts of God, should make a difference in how we operate on a day-to-day basis. These truths stay engrained in our minds when we accept the salvation Christ gives us.

The hope through the salvation we were freely given makes all the difference in how we face each day. The knowledge and truth of the forgiveness of our sins and the eternal life and love freely given to us is the truth that our brain can go to time and time again for protection when the world around us when we are under attack. This salvation truth makes a difference in our decision making, in how we treat others, in whether we have discernment or not, in whether or not we live day in and day out as God would have us; in whether or not we answer to His call. So, this helmet of salvation is something we need to remind ourselves everyday to stay clothed with – to operate out of – because it helps us in our daily battle as we work to continue to be the Women of God He calls us to be.

Think of it this way, when we put on the helmet of salvation, we put on Christ Himself. Christ protects not just our heads but our entire beings from spiritual death and also from painful attacks that could render us speechless, helpless, confused, dejected, feeling inferior, angry, making this mind an even greater battlefield as so many of us fight depression, anxiety and fear.

To wear the helmet of salvation means to live every day focused on eternity, knowing that what we see in front of us now is a poor reflection of the glory of the Lord and the future He has in store for those of us who believe. The helmet protects us from the whispers, the taunts, the lies of the enemy and preserves the truth within our minds that we have a future with the Lord that has been promised to us by a God who keeps His promises. When we walk around with this truth engrained inside us, life looks completely different. Hardships and pain look different. We see ourselves differently as well. Wearing the helmet of salvation means not merely existing, as if we're dead-women walking, carrying with us hopelessness about our existence like we're in a zombie apocalypse.

The helmet of salvation can also turn our eyes back to Jesus. There's a saying that goes, "When you fix your thoughts on God, God fixes your thoughts." (Buddy Owens) If your thought patterns are unhealthy, your ability to think clearly is fuzzy, and you're unable to make good decisions or follow the will of God, then something is broken and you need some good old fashioned fixing. **2 Corinthians 4:18** says, "[18] So we fix our eyes not on what is seen, but on what is unseen, since what is seen is temporary, but what is unseen is eternal." You have a shield of faith you can pick up to shield you from what you see coming at you and a helmet of salvation to help you focus on the unseen things that matter most. This armor will help remind you that though you cannot see eternity, you have been freely given eternal life through the death of Jesus on the cross.

Like the rest of the armor of God, you must pick up the helmet and wear it in order to stay protected. In doing so, you can fix your thoughts on Jesus. When you do, He will fix your thoughts. He will right the wrong thinking, shine the light of truth on the lies you believe and help get rid of the poor decision making, made outside His plan for you. The helmet helps protect you in this battle against your identity as the world of social media, entertainment, fashion, cosmetics, and plastic surgery beckons every woman to step into narcissistic vanity and pride so deeply that you change your physical appearance to match what the world says is beautiful rather than embracing the beautiful, unique woman God already made you to be. Wearing the helmet of salvation reminds us that we NEED this kind of protection from a world whose cultural 'reality' is far from real and from an enemy who is working overtime to destroy what the world thinks a real woman is. Yes, Women of God, our minds are a battlefield but take heart because we've been blessed with a full set of armor to fight the battle.

Using the helmet of salvation in the battle for your identity:

Putting on the helmet of salvation literally changes the way we live because it offers us more than future benefits via salvation and eternal life. Salvation is about more than saying "Hey, I belong to Christ so I'm going to heaven." It's about more than having a bumper sticker with a fish on it that quotes John 3:16 in the middle of it. Salvation, the knowledge of it, the truth and reality of it and the ability to put it on and use it as protection every single day is supposed to impact, not just our eternal future, but our present day walk. If we just go along and say "Yea, I have salvation through Jesus" and don't apply that truth and reality to our daily lives, or allowing it to affect how we operate, how we battle, what decisions we make, then we are taking the fullness of the helmet of salvation for granted.

When you're going about your day and the enemy strikes, do you shrink back, immediately getting angry or depressed, succumbing to the stress of the battle? Or do you operate out of the knowledge and the joy of your salvation? Do you remember that you have been blessed with protection and that you are who you are in Christ, a sinner who has been saved? .

This helmet of salvation - the ultimate head gear is always in fashion, by the way. It reminds us that salvation redeems us but it can also redeem our thinking. Do you find yourself allowing your mind to go to the negative? The inflammatory? The worst case scenario? Do you find yourself calling yourself names and putting yourself down? The helmet of salvation can help. Remember that Jesus died to save those He loves. You are one of His beloved. When you put down yourself, using harsh words and hurtful statements that are lies, you insult your Creator and leave yourself vulnerable to more lies being thrown at you about who you are because you have just shown the enemy that you're more than willing to embrace what he tells you about yourself. Remember, you are a Woman of God.

Woman of God, stand firm:

- Make a list of words, names and negative statements you find yourself saying about yourself throughout the coming week. Write them down. Every single one of them. Take each and every statement to the Lord in prayer and ask Him to reveal to you the truth or the lie in the statement and words that you wrote. If you write down "ugly", I know He will show you that you are beautiful. If you write down "lazy", He very well may reveal to you that you've been lazy in some area of your life but He will forgive you and give you energy and focus as you ask Him. If you write down "stupid", He will reveal to you the truth of your true intellect and wisdom. Whatever it is you find calling yourself or saying about yourself, pray in earnest for the Lord to open your eyes and take from you the lies you believe about who you are.

Note: This activity took me longer than a week. The lies I was believing and battling about who I am were deep and entrenched in my thinking. The years I've spent identifying my worth and who I am by how I looked, how much I weighed and by the attention or rejection of others, stole so much time from me. That was time I owed God, for there were many.

things I was called to do that I did not do, out of fear of rejection, anxiety over how I look and vanity. Processing that truth and allowing the Lord to show me what the lies were and why I believed them was a tearful, painful process but it helped me let go of so many falsehoods about who I am, allowing me to embrace my salvation and walk daily with my mind focused on things of heaven instead of stuff of earth.

- That activity may take you more than a week as well but I encourage you to set a time table so you don't slough it off and avoid doing it. Once you've completed the task, take your list and safely burn it. Put it in a fire pit, or a burn barrel or fireplace and watch the lies you have believed burn up as if on the flames of hell. Put a nail in the coffin of these lies that try to destroy your identity in Christ.

The sword of the Spirit

Ephesians 6:17 tells us to pick up the next piece of armor: "[17] ...the sword of the Spirit, which is the word of God."

Technically speaking, a Roman soldier could fight if he needed to without his helmet, without a shield and a breastplate but he could not fight without a sword. He would be a sitting duck, ready for slaughter. The type of sword most soldiers in Paul's day used was more like a very large knife, easy to wield, to swing around and to charge at the enemy with. It had 2 sharp edges. It was a double-edged sword and could do much damage to the enemy.

In verse 17, Paul references the sword of the Spirit as the final piece of armor, meaning the Holy Spirit wields the Word of God. This scripture says the sword is the Word of God. In order to understand greater the significance of this passage and how it helps us, we have to understand the significance and importance of the Word of God.

Hebrews 4:12 tells us "[12] For the word of God is alive and active. Sharper than any double-edged sword, it penetrates even to dividing soul and spirit, joints and marrow; it judges the thoughts and attitudes of the heart." This scripture is telling us that the Word of God helps us distinguish between what is right and wrong, to discern someone's attitude and thoughts, and to see what is of God and what is not of God. It is sharp enough to divide the joints from the marrow in our body. Now, that's a sharp piece of armor! Even the sharpest scalpel at a hospital cannot easily divide the bone from the marrow.

If we're lacking in knowledge and trust of God's Word then we are setting ourselves up to fall for any scheme the world has to offer and any attack of evil because we will not know truth from a lie. The Word of God is the truth and as I stated before, there is not my truth, or your truth, there is only THE truth. Truth combats lies. Truth combats fear because fear is all based in lies. So, in knowing the Word of God, carrying the sword of the Spirit, we have the very weapon in our hands that will shine a light on the lies of the enemy.

The sword of the Spirit is something that is housed inside the belt of truth. Within the truth you will find the Word of God. I love how Paul uses this imagery to remind us that the truth and the Word go hand in hand. The truth holds up the Word of God and keeps it in place and yet we have access to bring out the Word (the sword) and wield it as needed for our protection.

An interesting note on the sword of the spirit is how we are able to use it. In studying about the Word of God, I came across a compelling commentary from Biblestudytools.org. In their commentary about the armor of God, they bring us back to the scriptures. "The word Paul uses in Ephesians 6:17 for the "word" is rhema. The word rhema means "utterance" and refers to the spoken word. Scripture uses another word to describe the Word of God, and that word is logos. You see this in John 1:1, in which it refers to Jesus. What Paul is saying here is the sword of the Spirit is not just the written Word of God, but the written Word of God spoken directly into the conflict or battle you are facing. "

This means we have at our disposal, not only the written Word of God but the ability to speak out loud the Word of God over a battle in our lives and the living, active, powerful Word of God will have power over the attack. This truth goes along with what we're told in **2 Timothy 3:16**, "16 All Scripture is God-breathed and is useful for teaching, <u>rebuking</u>, correcting and training in righteousness,"

The written Word of God, when spoken out loud carries such power. As women of God we have been given power and authority to use the Word of God as protection against anything that comes up against us and threatens to steal and destroy our identity. A Roman soldier's sword was no small weapon and the sword of the Spirit is not minor in our arsenal either.

It's our job as women of God to use every bit of armor we've been blessed with. When you find yourself in a challenging situation where false words, temptations and attacks are happening, turn to the Word of God for protection and discernment. Speak the Word out loud over your situation.

Using the sword of the Spirit in the battle for your identity

If you don't have lots of scripture memorized that shouldn't stop you from accessing it. Keep a Bible with you or make sure you have a Bible app on your phone for quick reference. Not everyone has a sharp memory and the armor of God is offered to ALL who believe, not just those we have read the entire Bible and studied it for years. We all are given the opportunity to put on and take up the full armor of God, so carry yourself as a warrior and make sure you have the Word of God available at your fingertips and eventually it will become engrained in your heart, your thoughts, your memory and your everyday speech. Knowing what the Word says about who you are will help you battle the lies you believe. Having the Word at your fingertips, ready and willing to speak it over a situation and to check how what you're being told matches up to what God says, is essential in this battle for your identity. Hold up things spoken over you and about you to the magnifier that is the Word of God and it will give you a layer of protection from lies like nothing else can.

Woman of God, stand firm:

- Check your ability to access the Word of God. Do you use a smart phone frequently? Search for a quality Bible App and load it to your phone. You may not always have a good old fashioned Bible with you but most of us constantly have our phones. (Even in the bathroom…)

- Make sure you have a Bible in your car, at your work, in your office, in your living room and in your bedroom. (Yes, in all those places.) Bibles are $1 to $2 each at thrift stores or in used bookstores if you need more. Many churches give them away for free. Like many of you, I have a favorite Bible I use most of the time. You can tell by all the highlighted pages, tabs and sticky notes sticking out it which Bible I use the most. It's not the first one I've worn out. But I also keep Bibles in nearly every room because my memory isn't as good as it once was. Frankly, when I'm under attack, I also can't always remember a scripture that applies so I make sure the Word isn't far away so I can dig into it. I encourage you to do the same.

- Be on a quest to read from your Bible every single day. No exceptions. With a Bible every which way you turn in your world, there really are no excuses. Did you know that a study was done in 2019 by the Center for Bible Engagement. Go to the CenterforBibleengagement.org for more info and you will see that they polled 40,000 people and found that reading the Bible 4 times a week has a tremendous effect on your life.
Loneliness drops 30%
Anger issues drop 32%
Alcoholism drops 57%
Feeling spiritual stagnant drops 60%
Viewing porn drops 61%
Sharing your faith jumps 200%

Looking at this study, can you fathom the amazing effects the truth of the Word of God, the sword of the Spirit, will have on your identity and the war that is waged against it?

- Study the Word. If you are not part of a good Bible study group that meets at least a few times a month, find one! It can be in person or online. Face to face or virtual. Just find one. Reading the Word of our own accord every day is vital. But learning the true meanings and application of God's Word is just as important.

KAREN MCCRACKEN

THE POWER OF YOUR WORDS

I was in a small town in Kentucky not long ago where I went for a speaking engagement. It was a beautiful little town and the people were kind, gracious and family oriented. They were proud of their families. Entire families came to this conference together. I found that phenomenal. There were several generations from more than one family at the church conference. That's how they chose to spend their Saturday and Sunday. I don't think I've ever seen anything like that in all the years I've been speaking, and I've spoken all across the country, well over of 300 times in the past 25 years. This was amazing to me. I sat in a pew that had a woman in her 80's and with her was one of her daughters, and that daughter's granddaughter, along with one of her grandchildren, a great grandchild, and a great, great grandchild. They weren't the only family represented at this church conference in that way.

The other thing that struck me as interesting was the way they named their kids and/or generations of family members in this particular area. Let's say in was interesting.

Now, I've heard of people who name their kids after themselves or try to incorporate the mom or dad's name into the name of a child. Case in point, George Foreman. Yes, George Foreman the retired boxer, and evangelist. He named all his male children after himself. He named every one of his 5 sons George Edward Foreman. They all have the exact same name. No kidding. Now, they all have nicknames, which make me wonder why George named them all the same thing if he was going to let them go by their nicknames. He has 10 kids, 5 girls, 5 boys, all adults now. When someone asked him why he named them all the same thing he said, "I named all my sons George Edward Foreman so they would always have something in common," Foreman wrote on his website. "I say to them, 'If one of us goes up, then we all go up together. And if one goes down, we all go down together.'" I guess it keeps them on the straight and narrow because hey, if you're going to tarnish the George Foreman name, you'll have 5 other people to kick your booty because their names get tarnished too. He joked around when he was interviewed on Christian Broadcasting Network, saying, "I tell people, if you're going to get hit as many times as I've been hit by Mohammad Ali, Joe Frazier, Ken Norton and Evander Holyfield, you're not going to remember many names, so this helps me out.'" That made me giggle.

When I was in college, we lived next door to a family who had 5 kids. All the kids were named after their father in some way. James Jr., James Ella, Jamesina, Jody James, and Jamesy. Yes, I'm serious.

So, at this conference not long ago, one of the families I met had all 5 of their adult kids with them and their kid's kids as well. Their 5 adult kids were named Taylor, Teanna, Tyler, Toby, Tootie…AND –hold on – they called them Tay, Tea, Tye, Toe, Too. When I met them, one of them looked at me and pointed his thumb at his brother and said, "Yea, but it's easy to remember because we just call him stupid." None of the other siblings seemed to like that comment. He laughed. I know he was joking but it also triggered something inside me. It got me to thinking about name calling.

Now, I'm not going to go into some diatribe about sibling name calling and bullying in school. We all know that's wrong and if you don't, you need to be praying for God to reveal to you how

He sees it. This sibling's use of words and the conference conversation got me to thinking a bit more about name calling and the power our words have on other people. Right there, with one word being uttered – the word stupid – the whole conversation changed and the demeanor of most of the family changed from joyful to stressed.

Words matter. If identifying the Word of God as one of our pieces of armor isn't evident of that, I don't know what is. Words are powerful, and none more powerful than THE Word. But our personal words have power too, especially when we use them to call out, judge, and name call when what we should be doing is using them to affirm, uplift, edify and encourage others.

Unfortunately, I've gone through times when I call myself names rather than speak affirming words into my day. You know what I mean? Do you catch yourself doing the same thing? Maybe calling yourself negative things like stupid, ugly, lazy, or even worse? Our words have power to them. Degrading ourselves isn't a good or Godly thing to do but it's extremely easy to do. It's not okay for someone else to call you those things but we tend to justify it by cultural standards, don't we? If someone else called you a bad word, you'd get angry and yet you can call yourself the same thing and it's fine. People do it with relatives too. You can use your words against them and insult your own family but if anyone else does, you are likely to go off and get angry about it. We do not hold ourselves to the same standards we hold others to when it comes to using our words and name calling.

Last year I read a book called "The Hidden Messages in Water". It was a New York Times bestseller many years ago. It's written by a man who did studies on water and the effect words had on water, especially crystallized water. I know it sounds kind of strange but it's actually not. The man who did this is a Japanese scientist named Masaru Emoto and he discovered that the molecules of water are affected by our thoughts and words. Human beings have bodies that are composed mostly of water. Our bodies contain 60% water overall and the brain itself is composed of 73% water. In his book he talks not just about personal health and our environment but what affect words have on us as human beings and the fascinating way God made us. He's not pushy about God in the book but he definitely talks about a Creator. I don't know his faith beliefs but I plainly saw what his science represented.

I love it when science finally catches up with what those of us in the Body of Christ knew all along. If you read this book, know that it's not a Christian Biblical scriptural book but is categorized as a scientific book. Now, I personally know the Creator of the earth, who is the Creator of water, who also happens to be the Creator of human beings and the Creator of the sciences. Our Creator, our God, made us in such intricate, complex and amazing ways that I am always in awe and loving it when science comes along side faith and opens the eyes of those who do not understand how amazing His creation is.

I was interested to see what it was this book was talking about because for a long time I have seen in myself and in other people how our words affect our countenance. I wanted to see what their studies and research showed about how words affect water. I have seen for myself how our words affect our health, our immunity, diseases, and how our thoughts, words and attitude can create divisions in relationships, and predispose us to good or bad habits. There's a quote that says, "As a man thinketh, so shall he be." This actually comes from the New King James translation of **Proverbs 27:3** that says, "For as he thinks in his heart, so is he."

In this book, "The Hidden Messages in Water" the researchers take unbelievable close-up pictures of water crystallizations that have been subjected to different words and to music. Let me give you an example. The author and researcher shows up-close amazing photos of what happens to water crystals as they form when they're exposed to different kinds of music. The crystals that form when water is exposed to things like classical music such as Beethoven's 5th or 6th symphony or hymns are beautiful crystals. They're also different colors because different music causes them to be shaped differently and they refract light differently with each kind of music. Heavy metal rock creates a jagged and disfigured looking crystal.

In other experiments, he shows water that was spoken to and what those crystallizations looked like. He had children speak to the water and say positive things like, "You're so cute, you're adorable.", and then took pictures of the crystals afterwards. The crystals were adorable. They were cute. Then he had children talk to water, again during its crystallization process, and call it negative things such as "fool" and "stupid". The water formed strange oblong and round shaped crystal formations that were ugly when they used negative words.

These results were not random. These results happened 100% of the time. He did this time and time again with different kinds of music and different kinds of words. Every single time negative words and coarse sounding music was played, the crystals that formed were not symmetrical, not beautiful and were deformed.

If you're out on social media much there has been a home experiment similar to this that's been shown in various posts. You can do similar to what he talks about in his book. This is a trend online where people experiment using cooked rice. They start by putting the same amount of rice in two different jars, putting the lid on both and making sure it's tight. On one jar they put the label **hate** and on the other jar they put a label **love**. For two weeks they pick up the jars and say things to the jars. The hate jar they say negative and hateful things to. The jar that has the label that says love on it, they say loving and wonderful things to. (Yes, they're talking to rice.) The rice was first cooked in water before they put the rice in to the jars. The rice in each jar is from the same bag, cooked at the same time. Cooked rice is made up of 70% water, by the way. You put the jars on two different ends of your counter but in the same room, same temperature. The jar that has had hateful negative words spoken over it starts to turn black. The other jar does not. I have not tried this for myself but I've seen a lot of people on social media doing this.

These experiments and research brought me around to the thoughts of how powerful our own words are and what they do to us when spoken over us. Scientifically speaking, we are made of water. We are told in the Word of God that Jesus is THE Living Water and in Him we live and breathe and move and have life.

If you look around the world, people are hurting

and yet we live in a time, a season and a culture when words, written and spoken, have become weapons of war. In society today, women are being pummeled with words being spoken over us that absolutely affect our mindset, our viewpoint, and how we feel, mentally and physically. People are lashing out with horrible words and name calling. Suicide is at an all-time high in the United States and in other countries, mostly because of words. Words matter. If words didn't matter we wouldn't have THE Word of God. But we do have His Word and it is eternal. It is never changing and filled with the truth we need to fight the battles that threaten to destroy our identity.

My question to you is, are you name-calling? If you were a jar of rice would you be turning black? Would you have ugly crystallizations forming if you were water in that experiment? Or would you be beautiful, light-filled crystals, reflecting light?

So many of us have gotten caught up in the culture of self-hate and self-degradation; of comparing ourselves to everyone and everything that we have no business comparing ourselves to and then ridiculing ourselves because of it. I'm no different. Sadly, I've had times when I've just honestly felt completely worthless. Not long ago, literally three days in a row, I burned something while I was cooking dinner. I felt stupid and like I was a horrible cook. So, I called myself stupid and declared with my mouth that I was a horrible cook. I spoke those words over myself on the very first day. I did that on day one of three days of burning food. Now, if you just take the scientific principle that I am mostly made of water, physiologically speaking, what do you think those words did to the water in my body? Think of what that negatively charged water coursing through my body did to my brain and my organs?

Talking about this principle on a spiritual level, does it say anywhere in the Word of God that the Holy Spirit condemns us and leaves us for being flawed and making mistakes? Does it say anywhere in God's Word that He has declared that we human beings are stupid, ignorant, fat, ugly, worthless? No, it doesn't. In fact, the Word of God has many positive and wonderful things to say about His creation. **Proverbs 18:21** even says that "our words have the power of life and death." For me, the research done in that book on water, affirms what the Bible tells us. Our words have far more power than we give them credit for.

What we say about ourselves matters, just as much if not more, than what other people say about us. Someone else's opinion and their bullying or name calling hurts but it matters far less than what we say about ourselves. What matters most is if you know who you are; if you know that you are His and obedient to what He calls you to. That's the spiritual part right there. We are not merely flesh and bone or water, for that matter. If you know the truth of who you are in the Lord, and you know it without a shadow of a doubt, then no off key, off color, degrading reference that might start to come out of your mouth will change the composition of who you are - inside or out.

Remember that we have the ability to protect ourselves, to use the helmet of salvation to protect our minds and our brains from all the other stuff and junk that comes at us from other people. But we also have a responsibility to use the armor, the wisdom and the Word that God gave us to protect who we are from the negative connotations about ourselves that we allow to enter our brains and come out of our own mouths. I contend that we don't just have the responsibility to watch our words but when we don't do so, we are being disobedient. **Ephesians 4:29** says, "[29] Let no corrupt word proceed out of your mouth, but what is good for necessary edification, that it may impart grace to the hearers."

If we are not building others and ourselves up (edification) then we are bringing them and ourselves down. The Bible specifically talks about how we think about ourselves and the fact that it does affect us. It affects our path, our purpose and what we become. **Psalm 139:14** reminds us to check our thinking and our words: "I praise you, for I am fearfully and wonderfully made. Wonderful are your works; for my soul knows it very well." Your soul was created to know that you are a wonderful work of our Creator. When we aren't taught this, we wander and then we wonder who we are. When we are not affirmed by others and by scripture just who we are in Christ, we more easily choose to walk right past our armor, into the hands of the enemy who wants to make us speak powerful, negative words over ourselves.

1 Samuel 16:7 says, "But the Lord said to Samuel, "Do not look on his appearance or on the height of his stature, because I have rejected him." (Here is the key part.) "For the Lord sees not as man sees: man looks on the outward appearance, but the Lord looks on the heart."
I know it's difficult, not to get caught up in using self-deprecating words and degrading who you are. I truly do. This battle we fight against the darkness that wants to take over our identity is very real. It's a battle in which each Woman of God must choose to take up her armor and stand firm.

Women are being told we're not enough or we're too much. We're being told we're too thin or we're too fat. We're being told we need to go on this diet or that diet. We're being told we're not making enough money or we're focusing on it too much. Everywhere you look, including in many churches, we're being told we're not enough and there's something wrong with us. The only thing wrong with us is that we are flawed, imperfect human beings who were born with a sin nature like everyone else. But we have a Savior who has taken care of that for us, praise Him.

We were created in God's image. He's perfect and we are not but over time we are being perfected in Him, meaning that through His grace and atonement for our sins we have the opportunity to become whole and complete. I have to remind myself of this almost daily. Sometimes I forget that I was made in His image. When I feel down about myself, or someone has insulted me and I want to believe what they said, I tend to go on a tangent of berating myself, using negative words against myself. I question myself with negativity. Am I too much? Do I look right? Should I wear make up? Am I wearing the right kind of clothing? Are my clothes too baggy? Are my clothes too tight? And all of those thoughts cause me to want to sit and insult myself. They tempt me to become the jar on the counter whose rice is turning black because negative words are constantly being spoken over it. I have to be diligent to remind myself what it says in **Genesis 1:27**, "So God created man in his own image, in the image of God he created him; male and female he created them."

There's an old quote I've heard many people quote though I don't know the original source. It goes, "God didn't make no junk." Horrible grammar but the saying is true. He didn't make junk. He made each of us how we are for a reason. Yes, we have to take care of ourselves but that means not just our physical health but spiritually, mentally and emotionally as well. We're all made in God's image and yet we each were made differently. Now, if that doesn't tell you what an amazing God we have, I don't know what else will. We all have things in common and yet we all look different from each other. (Unless you're an identical twin.) Yes, we have similarities in our individual families but when it comes down to it, inside and out we were all made differently even though we all have one Creator, one Father, and we were made in His image.

I don't know if I put a jar of rice on the counter and say bad things to it if it's going to turn black or not. But I know how I feel after I have done some name calling. I almost feel dark inside. After I've gone on a tangent about how horrible I am, I feel worse. If I continue that kind of negative self-talk, it affects every part of me for days on end.

I heard many years ago when I was in college, taking classes on psychology and psychiatry, that for every negative word someone hears about themselves it takes a thousand positive ones to rewrite that thought in their brain. If we're going to do name-calling, then we need to do name-calling that comes straight from the Word of God because we know that in His Word is truth. Then we can rewrite all those negative things that are stuck in our brains and erase the lies, replacing them with truth. His truth is a truth we can stand firm on, stand upright in and share with others.

Women of God, the truth is, I'm not stupid. Neither are you. Sometimes I feel like I'm stupid because I do things that make no sense or I don't do something right or I simply forget things. But I'm not stupid. I am not unloved. I'm not less than, not worthless or a failure because I'm a plus-sized woman most of the time. I'm not more valuable when I go down 3 sizes and I'm not less valuable when I go to the store wearing sweats and a t-shirt with my hair in an old fashioned scrunchy. Believing falsehoods like those or saying those negative words over myself only gives Satan a foothold to further degrade me, distract me from what God calls me to do and allows Satan one step closer to a full-on assault against my identity.

I know how difficult it is to wrap our brains around the fact that we were made preciously, purposefully and with a plan. As flawed as we feel, as ugly as we feel at times, as imperfect as we are, we were made just as we are, by a perfect Creator, for a precise purpose. I don't like all the aches and pains in my body; I don't like the fact that as I get older I have less hair, more chins and a harder time remembering things. I don't like that sometimes I care what other people think of me. And other times I could care less. Somewhere in there is the truth that what I should care about is purely what my Heavenly Father thinks of me and what I need to know is who I am in Him; that I am His and I am redeemed.

I am who God made me to be and you are who God made you to be. Not sure who that is? Then please take some time with the Lord to dig deeper into it. If you're in a habit of labeling yourself negative things or you make your immediate reaction to difficult situations one that has you speaking negative words over yourself, then I implore you to take some time to dig into the Word of God and find out who you really are and let those positive words and truths write over the lies that you've believed and ended up telling yourself.

Woman of God, stand firm:

- Every time you come up with a negative word or a name that you want to call yourself because you feel horrible in the moment, I want you to think about what that does, and what that says about your relationship with the One who made you. How insulting are you being to Him when you are degrading what He made and who He made you to be?

- Think about the experiment with the water the next time you feel down about who you are, how you look and where you are in life today. What are you doing to yourself inside and out every time you heap negative thoughts and bad names upon yourself?

- Find out the truth of who you are through His Word and find out for yourself that you are loved by a God who made you just the way you are for a reason, maybe even a reason you cannot fathom at this point in time but take heart and know that you were made for a purpose.

Let me start you out with these verses (find a Bible or open an app):

If you call yourself weak and wimpy. "God arms me with strength, and he makes my way perfect" - **Psalm 18:32**

If you say you're a sinner and that's all you'll ever be, **1 John 2:12** says otherwise.

If you say you're alone and will always be alone, **Joshua 1:9** says, "God is with you wherever you go."

John 15 tells us that you are justified and redeemed, you are forgiven, you are a friend of Jesus, you are a branch from the true Vine, you're accepted by Christ, and you are to be called a saint.

1 Corinthians 1:30, shares with us that in Christ Jesus, you have wisdom, righteousness, sanctification, and redemption.

Jeremiah 31:3 tells each of us that, "The LORD appeared to us in the past, saying: "I have loved you with an everlasting love; I have drawn you with unfailing kindness."

LET GO OF THE BAGGAGE

LET GO OF THE BAGGAGE

I heard someone on TV in a comedy show say not long ago, "It ain't baggage if you refuse to pick it up and carry it with you." Pardon the poor grammar, Mom. I was raised in the era of "Ain't, ain't a word" but many people today accept it as a common. In fact, it is now in most dictionaries, including Miriam Webster although there is a foot note that says "Ain't is disapproved of in many circles." If one of those circles includes mothers in their 80's, then you're bound to find mine there. But for the purposes of this quote, we will henceforth consider ain't a real word...at least until the last chapter is completed and published.

So, this quote: "It ain't baggage if you refuse to pick it up and carry it with you", it struck me like lightning strikes that man in South Carolina who's been hit by lightning 11 times in his life. They say lightning never strikes twice but I've never heard them say that it doesn't strike 11 or 12 times, so I'm guessing he probably ought to watch out. That man defied all the odds by being struck by lightning more than once and by living to tell about it all 11 times. His wife says she never gets near him in a storm, for self protection and well, so someone can be around to call 911 when he gets hit. Smart woman.

What about this quote about baggage and the whole idea of picking up that baggage? What does that have to do with your identity and this battle for it? And do you actually have the freedom not to claim that baggage as yours in the first place? Or are we obligated to hold on to the past's mistakes and issues?

Good news. As it turns out, we are not obligated to hold on to the past and in fact, it would be mentally, emotionally, spiritually and physically far less harmful to us if we didn't hold on to baggage. When we choose to see our past as something we must hold on to in the present day and even drag with us into the future, we have just created a weakness in our armor. Think of it this way, when the scripture in Ephesians tells us to "take up the full armor of God", it's serious. (**Ephesians 6:10-18**) But imagine for a moment a soldier, a Knight from days of old or a modern day police officer. As he or she steps in to battle the foe, how would a soldier draw his sword if he is carrying a back pack filled with heavy items and dragging an overloaded suitcase? Can you picture it? Realistically thinking, if a soldier was confronted by the enemy, in order to defend himself he must be able to draw his sword. This is nearly impossible if he's weighted down with baggage he's taking along with him.

I see people struggle, saying they're armored up when all the while they're carrying years of old baggage right along with them into the spiritual battle of their life. It makes us weak and susceptible to being clobbered. We're given armor for a reason but it's up to us if we use it or not. I've seen and heard many a sermon on the armor of God but never have I heard a Pastor, Preacher or Speaker say, "You must add a Louis Vuitton clutch purse, a gym bag and some carry-on luggage to your armor." There's a reason for that. When we hold on to the worldly idea that we're able to fight our battles while being distracted with old baggage, then we lose. We get pummeled. When we hold onto the past person we were, the hurts we endured, the pain we caused, unforgiveness we stubbornly won't relinquish, then we have weighed ourselves down and sent up a white flag to the enemy letting Satan know that he can throw every lie at us about who he thinks we are and we will believe it. We cause ourselves to become mentally and emotionally weak when we hold on to what we were or who we thought we were, instead of who we truly are in the Lord.

As is with most things God needs to smack me in the face with, this truth came at just the right time. I may not always understand why I'm getting smacked with something in the moment but I usually figure it out before long. If I don't see it as applicable in the moment, I know that God is preparing me for something headed my way, as was the case with this baggage quote. God's good to me like that, even though I don't deserve it. He knows what's coming up for each of us. He prepares us in ways we might not be able to see or in ways that drive us crazy in the moment but help us in invaluable ways when we get to the part of 'going through' whatever it is He knew we needed to prepare for. I know there's a phrase about being Gob smacked but this is totally different. Being Gob smacked is a British and Scottish term for being totally shocked or astonished. For me, God-smacked is more appropriate and much deeper than that. It can be a surprising, shocking, astonishing moment, yet it's deeper. It's one of those things that makes you think, feel or say "no way" or "Oh, my gosh, I get it!" It lingers, it lasts and stays with you for longer than something that just gob smacks you – it's not a mere feeling, it's like being struck by spiritual lightning. That's what I call being God-smacked.

So one day I was God-smacked by that quote. "It ain't baggage if you refuse to pick it up and carry it with you." I was God-smacked not because I hate the word ain't but because it hit me right where I needed it to. It sunk in a bit and then a few days later, really smacked and struck me hard. I needed to know this information. I needed to be able to go back to it over and over again for days in order to heed its warning and work to apply it to my journey.

Not sure about you, but I have done my fair share of picking up things along this journey and carrying them with me. I've taken full ownership as if I had a claim ticket and picked them up at baggage claim. What things? Things like people, experiences, mistakes, hurts, pains. All of these were things I had no business picking up and holding on to. They've weighed me down. The weight of carrying all these little boxes, bags and emotional totes, drug me down to a place of constant anxiety, with fear scratching on the surface of daily life. Every- single- day. It's really something I'd done since I was younger. I'm not sure why. Was it something I saw my parents do? Probably. When they were younger I'm sure they did similarly. As they got older, I didn't see it as much. I know my Dad had told me many times before he passed away that it was better to let go of things than to carry them with you, which includes people. He had learned over his lifetime that sometimes he had to love people at a distance. He had to let them go because it wasn't healthy for him to have them in his life. That's something I try hard to remember but don't always practice well.

Sometimes we don't let go of baggage in the form of things or people because we're afraid to hurt others in the process of the letting go. OR we don't let go because IF we let go, that means letting go of control and there's a whole lot of us who have control issues. But in the end, as difficult as it is, I'm happier, less anxious and more peaceful when I let go of the things and people I should. One thing is for sure, if I've held on to someone or something too long, it then causes me to sin and I more easily lose my temper, cuss, make rash and poor decisions. I know without a shadow of a doubt that it's been too long and I've been holding on to old baggage if I get to that point. The expiration date has come and gone. That relationship or situation is far past the "best if used by" date when it triggers me to operate out of a position of anger and sin. When the baggage I'm carrying causes me to act as if I either don't know who I am or it changes who I am in a negative way, that means I am long past the point of needing to discard the baggage and, I have not picked up my armor. I picked up that old baggage instead.

Sound harsh that I'm talking about a person or people as baggage that weighs us down? Perhaps, but I think you just might understand exactly where I'm coming from. Maybe you're there now. Maybe you've allowed someone in your life to become a weight that is too heavy for you to carry but you're ashamed or afraid to address it? That person or situation has become a true heavy load you can no longer carry; making you wish you could drop that load. Well, perhaps it's time to set down the baggage and pick up your armor instead. Prune the trees, clean the vine. Throw off the dead weight. Take some time and pray about it. Ask God to show you. Is it some relationship that's dying or long dead? Or some connection from the past you've put on the back burner but the weight of it is becoming too heavy of a load? If you look at a dead tree limb, or dead vines, you can see them shrivel, get harder, and they eventually cease to bear fruit or grow leaves. Dead weight is simply like that, dead. You are called to live – to be alive while you're breathing – spiritually, mentally and emotionally alive while your body is still here. You're called to walk the walk the Lord has laid out for you according to His will and His purpose. That's hard to do when you're carrying around old baggage and dead weight.

The Bible tells us that God prunes back the branches that are alive and bear fruit so they will bear more fruit. Hopefully you're bearing fruit for Him. Hopefully you're growing and filled with life. The Bible also says in **John 15:1-3** that He cuts off and disposes of the dead branches that bear no fruit at all. That's not just a warning for us but also an example. If we allow someone else's dead weight to pull us down then we are susceptible to ceasing to bear fruit as well. If we allow something or someone, a relationship maybe, that is dying or dead, to cling to us and suck the life out of us, we are stepping towards spiritual and emotional death ourselves.

Do you have someone like that in your life? Someone you know full well that God has shown you, you should not be in relationship with? Yet you fear hurting him or her? Or you hate confrontation or you are hooked on the drama they bring? Maybe you're one of those people who feed off that passive aggressive, toy with my emotions drama or the highs and lows that come from that kind of a half-dead, draining relationship. Sounds odd but there are people who were born and raised in chaos and drama who actually seek it out or let it linger because it seems "normal" to them. Chaotic comfort...that might be a good phrase for it. Chaotic comfort. But God has SO much more in mind for you than distractions, unhealthy relationships and energy sucking activities you do out of feeling obligated. He wants you to live and breathe and move in Him. And when you do, you will know more fully who you are in the Lord.

John 15: 2- 4 says, "2He cuts off every branch of mine that doesn't produce fruit, and he prunes the branches that do bear fruit so they will produce even more. 3 You have already been pruned and purified by the message I have given you. 4 Remain in me, and I will remain in you. For a branch cannot produce fruit if it is severed from the vine, and you cannot be fruitful unless you remain in me."

Sometimes it hurts when God prunes us. Sometimes He cuts things out of our lives and prunes back our responsibilities or luxuries or even our desires that we didn't want to get rid of and we might not understand why in the moment. But He always has a plan. Again, He sees what you can't see. He knows what you need before you even do. Sometimes He calls us to prune; to let go of the dead limbs, the baggage from the past and the lies we believe that tell us we are something we are not. We are called to pick up those shears for ourselves at times and cut off or cut out the dead weight so we can bear fruit.

I've found from my own experiences, that if I keep things that tend to distract me from my purpose regularly trimmed up, pruned back and refuse to carry any dead weight, then God doesn't have to do as much for me in the way of forcing me to let go. Yes, I need pruning at times when I don't even realize it because I slip, don't take care of my spiritual and emotional needs or relationships as I should, or because I just plain can't see what's coming my way. But He sees! And so when He prunes, I have to accept it and work hard to know, inside and out, that it's for my best. But there are many times when I've allowed someone or something into my life and I know without a doubt that I have to cut them out, set them down and not carry them because He calls me to stay healthy. He calls me to have relationships that honor Him and that allow me to bear fruit and to truly live, rather than pull me one step closer to spiritual death. I have to be cautious and only allow close relationships, activities, and hobbies that affirm who I am in the Lord, not ones that cause me to doubt or question the truth.

So, after hearing this quote about not picking things up and carrying them, I had an emotional tug of war go on inside me over an unhealthy relationship in my life. This is someone who has hurt me before. While they can be well-meaning, they are also very much about what they want, what they need, what they think and what their own world view is. As I was reminded, God puts people in our lives for reasons and for seasons. Sometimes it's time to let the season pass and let those people go. I was also reminded, after much hurt, that the hurt and pain and the season passing probably wasn't all about me. In a relationship we tend to think about ourselves first and foremost and sometimes we only think about the me, me, me aspect. I've come to realize that often times when I have to let go of someone, it's as much or more about them as it is me. If my purpose in their life has run its course and I've fulfilled what God called me to do for that person, then I have to accept that it's all buttoned up and I need to move on. I need to let go of the baggage I claimed from that relationship and move on. Not just for myself but for that person as well.

One thing I can do that helps me stay in tune with these times and understand when and how I'm supposed to let go of people is to read the Bible. It also helps me purge the baggage that weighs me down and that causes me to doubt who I am in the Lord. I have to keep in His Word to keep sharp about what God wants from me and what He doesn't. I need to stay in regular

KAREN MCCRACKEN

prayer and praise to Him. This also helps me to discern who and what I should or shouldn't allow in my life in the first place. In other words, if I start by not picking up the baggage in the first place, I'm far better off and way ahead of the game!

Like that comment I heard someone say the other day: "It ain't baggage if you refuse to pick it up and carry it with you", when something becomes seemingly dead weight or I'm supposed to let something or someone go, I've learned that I have to do it or whomever or whatever it is, becomes baggage. If I say "no" to God, and insist on saying "yes" to carrying whatever it is I know He doesn't want me to carry, then I ain't got no one to blame but myself! (Pardon the language.)

When I seriously analyze and think about the times in my life when I was working hard to stay in a relationship or go down a particular path to accomplish something that I knew was outside of His plan for me, there seemed to be blockades every which way I turned and those things I wanted typically never came to fruition. That was God's protection. I believe God put all those road blocks in the way for me so I didn't veer off my path and go a way I wasn't supposed to go. It's when I'd charge those blockades and push my way through that I'd gather things, people and experiences I was never meant to have. He sees up ahead where we cannot though and I have to use my armor in order to fight the enemy who wants me to veer off course. God knows that some people and experiences I want to push my way towards will cause me to doubt who I am or make me think I need to go outside God's plan for my life, so He protects me. It's my job not to reject the ways God wishes to protect.

Pruning and letting go

Let me clarify here that just because God calls you to do it; to let go of someone or something, it doesn't mean it will necessarily be easy. It may take some time. Maybe you do need to get rid of baggage you've been carrying for a long time that you never should have picked up in the first place. It might take a bit more time to get rid of the baggage you half-heartedly picked up yet let get into your head about who you are. It's imperative that you stop the infestation that you allowed to gradually change the definition of who you are though. Yes, seeds of lies and doubt are almost like an infestation or a weed that grows trying to take over the truth. Maybe you are indeed called to prune back that thing, that habit that desire, that person so he, she or it doesn't continue to plant seeds that blossom into weeds and become a heavy dead weight you're carrying. Pruning can take time, so take heart, be armored up and hold on. You can't just rip something or someone from you without likely creating deeper wounds at times so hold on to the strength the Lord has for you. Seek wisdom and strength to do it. Seek God to show you when and how to prune back, to let go and do it in a way that's healthy for you. Seek the guidance and comfort of the Holy Spirit through these processes.

You know, when I think about trying to carry something we shouldn't carry, I think about my nephew. When he was about 6 years old he tried to pick up my Dad, his grandfather. He had seen a superhero show and on the show this strong superhero had lifted a man up with one hand. My nephew was playing superhero so he wanted to try to lift my dad up. A tiny little 6 year old boy trying to lift a full grown man! But my nephew was determined. He grabbed one leg and started trying to lift and lift. It was so cute. The look of determination on his face was sweet and inspiring as he grunted and groaned trying to get his grandfather lifted up off the ground. Unable to budge his grandfather, he then wrapped both his arms around my dad's legs and tried to lift him that way. He huffed and puffed but all he did was knock my dad off balance a little bit. He tried grabbing my Dad's socks and his shoes but to no avail. Finally after we were all giggling like crazy my nephew stood up, put his hands on his hips and said, "That's not fair, you're pushing down too hard!" As if my Dad pushing down was the issue, not the fact that a tiny 6 year old was trying to lift the full weight of a grown man. We all laughed.

When I recall that memory, I think that sometimes we must look like that to God. Here we are grunting and groaning, huffing and puffing, trying to lift and carrying things we are not strong enough to carry on our own and have no business trying to life or take along with us on this journey.

"That supernatural fatigue you're carrying around with you right now is dead weight of the past and you seem to insist on dragging it into the future." That's a quote I love by Emma Magenta. Have you ever felt that way? That you're carrying baggage around with you that brings you down spiritually and mentally? And yet, we continue to carry it, dragging it into our future relationships and goals with us.

What have you picked up and brought along with you that you should be putting down? Is there anything or anyone? Is it your past decisions, mistakes and choices? What are you carrying that you're supposed to let go of? Has it caused you fatigue? Has it caused you to become confused about who you are or what your purpose is? Do you feel weighed down by it - spiritually, emotionally and mentally fatigued?

Woman of God, stand firm:

- Take time now to spend one on one time with God to seek His direction on the matter. Ask of our Lord what it is He wants you to put down, prune back, purge and drop. Find out and then seek His strength to follow through in doing so. Once you do, you will feel lighter, freer and strengthened. You'll have more energy to stay armored up when you refuse to pick the baggage up at the same time as the armor

TO IMPRESS OR TO IMPACT

If your heart belongs to something or someone other than God, then you will seek to make an impression. If your heart belongs to God, you will seek to make an impact.

By now, hopefully you know that in order to know who you are you have to know whose you are. If you belong to God, heart, mind, body, soul, attitude, actions and words, then you will seek to make an impact for the Kingdom of God rather than impress those operating in and for the world.

There is a quote by Nancy DeMoss I love that says, "Our greatest effectiveness is not in being like the world. It is found in being distinct from the world. It is found in being Christ-like."

I contend that if you're trying to impress the

people around you, whether they're in your family or friend group, at church or on the job, then you have let the priority of living a life Jesus wants you to live, go to the wayside. You have things backwards. Jesus didn't call us to impress others. He called us to make an impact.

Are you one to sit and wonder what kind of an impression you've made on someone? Most of us have wondered about far more than a time to two in our lives. Some people altogether don't care what kind of an impression they make on others. I might say I'm one of those people who doesn't care because I've frankly worked hard not to care what most people think of me. Let me be frank though when I tell you that not caring so much what others think of me can be extremely difficult. Not impossible, but most definitely difficult. Especially people I love who are supposed to love me, accept me, embrace me, according to family connection, that is. Friends I've known for what seems like forever are also difficult not to want to impress or please, and yet, there are people who don't accept me or embrace me and would rather I really not leave any impression on them whatsoever. Are you in that same boat? People pleasing, begging for attention, connection and love from family or friends who once loved you but have discarded you? I believe it's epidemic.

I spoke at a church in Indiana once and after the

first session a woman came forward to ask if I'd pray with her. I had shared with the women in the first session about a family member I had been led to disconnect from. It's someone I sought out time and time again for years but who rarely ever made time for me, only occasionally supported me in anything I did and decidedly couldn't tell the truth if someone paid her to. After being hurt time and time again, I finally had to let that person go and leave that relationship to the Lord. I had to stop putting her before the things God called me to do.

At one point this person blew up at me over the phone because she didn't want me praying for her. She couldn't stop me from praying for her but her actions did stop me from reaching out to her again for a very long time. I realized when her actions caused me to want to sin, lash out, cuss, scream and feel a sense of hatred that I had to distance myself from that kind of toxic relationship.

Even though I've never had the kind of relationship I once wanted with this relative, I'm thankful I got to the point where I could see that if I was reaching out, trying to impress this person, rather than make an impact, it was never going to work. She was never going to be impressed by me. She was never going to understand me. I also learned that in changing and morphing who I was to please her, I was displeasing God.

The woman who asked me to pray for her at that church in Indiana had encountered a similar situation and was hurting. She had allowed that hurt, much like I did for a long time, to dictate her actions and change who she was to impress a person who never took the time to make their friendship work.

I don't know anyone who doesn't encounter rejection like this woman and I have. Sometimes out and out nasty attitudes tend to take over our common sense when we've been hurt time and time again. To say that I had let the hurt and pain of rejection change who I was, was an understatement. Like the quote by Nancy Demoss says, "Our greatest effectiveness is not in being like the world. It is found in being distinct from the world. It is found in being Christ-like." Make no mistake about it, I was not being Christ-like towards this person after years of rejection and hurt coming my way.

If you're in a place where you find yourself acting unChrist-like toward someone, please take the time to pray, to wake up, and to focus more on making an impact rather than trying to impress them. Those are the kinds of hurts we have to leave at the foot of the cross, in God's hands to deal with, and then embrace an attitude of "It doesn't matter what they think of me. I am not called to impress. It matters what God thinks of me and if I'm doing what He calls me to do. That's what will make an impact."

So, in taking about what kind of an impression you leave on others, I'm not just talking about the people who know you intimately, or those who love you and embrace you (or should but don't). I'm talking about the people you meet in a brief exchange at the store, or via customer service on the phone, or in the middle of a crowded airport, in a business meeting, at a new group gathering, in the local gift shop or in the drive-thru at the bank or working at the coffee shop. Those impressions; the brief, barely have time to utter a word or roll your eyes kind of impressions also matter. These are the type of brief impressions that could make an impact in ways you can't imagine. These small, everyday encounters are amazing moments where we who are God's children, are called to make a sudden impact, plant seeds and show the love of Christ in small ways that can make a big difference.

Let me ask a different question. Have you ever wondered if you're making a lasting impact? If what you say and do, or your very presence, ever makes an impact on someone else's life? Do you think that anyone you've met has ever walked away thinking, "Wow" or "Hmmm" or "Thank you, Jesus" or I don't know, maybe even "Not today, Satan?" Hopefully not the latter, although

I'm sure we've all had days when we maybe acted like a little devil because we didn't check our attitude at the door. Surely, I'm not alone in falling short.

One-time years ago when I was taking flyers from store front to store front for the school I was working for, I entered one of those cash advance check-cashing stores. When I entered, the woman behind the counter was arguing with the man who was in line in front of me. There was only one person in line besides myself. I saw no one else in the store. I kind of stayed towards the back of the storefront closer to the door, unsure of what was going on. I was afraid it was some sort of robbery or something. I had no idea. But they had words and he stormed out. As I slowly approached the counter, I could tell she was upset. I just stood there and waited for her to look up. When she did, she said loudly and in an aggravated tone, "What?" I'm sure I winced a little. I was definitely surprised by her tone. I looked at her and said, "Pardon me but these are the flyers the school said they'd send over." She said, "Fine. Give them to me." As I handed them to her, she just froze. She stared off into space and blanked out. I said, "Are you okay?" She didn't answer me. She just looked at me like she had no idea what I was saying. I said, "Is there something I can do for you? Are you okay?" and she kind of looked like she had just woken up. She said pretty harshly, "Yes, why? Don't I look okay? Why do you care?" In that moment I thought, "Wow, is she the spawn of Satan?" Then I thought, "No, something is wrong. Be Christ-like." (Yes, I have to remind myself of this frequently. You're not alone in that.) I was tempted to snap back something sarcastic and nasty to her. But I didn't. I just looked at her and said. "No, you don't look okay. You look like something's wrong, and I'm concerned. Are you okay? Do you need help in some way?" In an instant her whole demeanor changed. She softened. Her face looked less rigid, her shoulders relaxed. She said, "No. I'm okay, really. It's just been a very bad day. I'm sorry."

Not sure about her but she made a lasting impression on me, and I believe if even for one moment of her day, I made a positive impact on her. That memory sticks with me because I've rarely had anyone be so defensive over me simply asking if they were okay. Truthfully, most of the time we have no idea what kind of impression or impact we might make on someone else's life but what we can know is that when we operate out of the knowledge of who we are in Christ and act accordingly, we will make an impact for the Kingdom of God. Even the briefest of exchanges or a temporary relationship of some sort can make an impact.

The Bible says in **Hebrews 13:2** that when we show hospitality and entertain strangers we might just be entertaining angels. According to the account in **Genesis 19**, Lot was sitting at the gate of the city one evening when two unidentified strangers came along. Without knowing who they were, he invited them to his home for a night's rest, and later learned that they were angels. So, there are examples in the Bible of treating others in a Godly manner, whether we know them or not. We don't have to go searching at the end of the road to invite a stranger over for dinner or do a song and dance to entertain them because that's not what the passage in **Hebrews 13** means. This passage in Hebrews is talking about making an impact. It's telling us that you never know who you might be helping or who you might be being kind to or showing love to. It could be a messenger from God. It could be someone in great need. It could be someone who has never heard The Word of God or been shown kindness or love before.

This also makes me think about the woman at the well. In the Bible it talks about how the woman at the well had a lengthy conversation with Jesus even though she didn't know he was the Messiah at the time. As we can tell from those verses in John 4, there is no doubt Jesus made an impact on her.

Once you walk away or end your day, lying down to get some shut-eye, you truly have no idea whether or not what you've said or done in the presence of others has made an impact at all, good or bad. I don't pretend to know how much of an impact I made on the woman at the check-cashing store but I don't need to know. I just need to be content to know that if I'm operating out of the knowledge of who I am in the Lord and how He wants me to act, then my obedience will be honored. This is one way I am able to help make a positive impact on the world and eventually the seeds I plant will one day grow and hopefully a harvest will be reaped.

There are other times when you may plant a seed or show a kindness towards someone out of your obedience and then through the grace of God you find out that you did indeed make an impact. This happened to me about 22 years ago when I found out that something I had done made a huge impact on not just one person but several. It was one small thing I did that I just felt led to do in the moment. The only person I told about it at the time was my husband.

It was a crazy, rainy day outside. Dark, cloudy and periods of utter downpours were happening. It was the kind of rain that soaks you from head to toe in an instant. It literally hurt my head when I stood out in it. Now, I wasn't purposefully standing out in the rain getting soaked, but I had come from an appointment and had to be out driving in it. As I went down a pretty busy main street I saw two women walking in the rain. They had plastic grocery bags over their heads. I thought, "Oh no, this is horrible. " They looked like one of those cartoons where the characters are just pummeled as they walk in the rain? The wind was blowing their coats and their scarves back. I slowed down, went a few streets past them, turning around to go find them to see if I could give them a ride to wherever they were going.

I don't normally pick up people I don't know and take them some place but as soon as I saw them, I knew I had to. I actually tried to keep driving straight on home, but God just kept bringing them to my mind like rapid fire. So, I prayed, turned around and tried to find them. After I'd driven awhile looking down several streets I decided to give up. I couldn't find them. I finally decided they'd either been picked up by someone else or stopped in a business to wait for the worst of it to pass. I turned down a side street and made a U-turn to head home. When I turned around, there they were, walking down the side street. I pulled over in front of them and got out with my umbrella. They were a bit nervous, I'm sure because I was a stranger. I would have been too. But the rain was just coming down like cats and dogs, screaming and barking at us, so they didn't bolt. They waited for me to speak.

I offered them a ride to wherever they were going. One of the ladies looked like she was in her 60s and the other was slightly older. The younger said that she was taking her friend to the doctor and she pointed to the building about 200 feet from where we stood. I told her I could drive them, and she said she didn't want to get inside my car since she was so wet. I assured her it was fine. But she said, "No, thank you." Then in an instant I said, "Here, at least take my umbrella." And she said "Oh no, that looks expensive." She was right. It was expensive. It was one of those fancy extra large golf umbrellas. I told her it didn't matter and gave it to her. I could tell she was touched. She was so thankful. She tried to get my phone number so she could call me and send me money or return it and I told her it wasn't necessary. I was frankly getting more and more soaked so I just wanted to do what I felt led to do and go on my way. I asked her to please take the umbrella. She finally agreed. Once back in my car I sat and waited as they walked that 200 feet to the building, making sure they were okay.

About 2 weeks later my husband, cousin and I were at a church fellowship with about 75 other people. The youth pastor said he had to share something that really touched him. He said a friend of his told him about his neighbor's grandmother. She and her friend were trying to get to the doctor's office a couple weeks ago when it rained like crazy. They were freezing and yet they didn't have transportation, so they'd prayed for God to help them get to the doctor and for Him to protect them. They ended up caught in the middle of a downpour when a delivery truck of some sort went speeding by and splashed water up so hard that they became soaked. So, as they walked, they prayed. Just a short way from their destination, a woman pulled over, offered them a ride and gave them her umbrella. She refused to take money for it and she made sure they got to the building safely. The youth pastor said, "I was so touched. Here in a day and age when people just want to take, take, take, there was someone, out of the goodness of their heart, who stopped to simply be kind and help their neighbor, not asking for anything in return." He said, "That's how I want to be. That's the kind of person I want to be like…Christ-like, impacting others with simple, everyday kindness and love others like Jesus did."

I was stunned. I was touched, and I was reminded, that even when we think others aren't watching, God always is. He is paying attention to what we say, do, and of course, to how we present ourselves to a world that needs His hands and feet to make an impact. God knows I almost didn't turn around that day. He knows that I had a slight attitude at first, but He also knows that my heart softened, and I desired to show those ladies how much I cared. What I didn't know was that this small Christ-like gesture would make such a big impact. I didn't just make a lasting impression and I didn't set out to impress the world. I made an impact; a Christ-like impact. I did so because of who I am in the Lord and who He made me to be. Had I not known that He made me as I am for a reason, I would not have been obedient to His call to help those ladies in the downpour that day. I would have had no need to challenge myself, nor do away with my initial attitude of not wanting to be inconvenienced

That small pebble I threw in the water sent ripples out far beyond what I could imagine. I feel blessed that I was able to hear some of the impact my small gesture had. That little old me, who used to be afraid of my own shadow at times, was able to touch and motivate someone else to try harder to entertain angels unaware, to be more Christ-like in the ordinary day in and day out, touched me in ways it's hard to express.

Fast forward 22 years and these days with social media's reach you have a greater chance of knowing if you're doing a good job or not because you never know who is lurking or lingering near to catch you on a video. And if you're captured doing something Godly or positive you just might be able to go out and read the positive comments and suggestions from people as well as any nasty remarks others wish to add. But on a day-to-day basis, most of us don't get that kind of feedback and I believe that's a good thing. The more we operate and make daily decisions out of who we are in the Lord, instead of for attention, likes and feedback, the greater our faith grows. When it comes down to it, it's all a matter of faith anyhow. You do because you're called to do. You may make an impression that's hopefully a good one, but the point is not to impress, it's to use who you are in the Lord to make an impact.

The word impact means, "to come into contact with another person and to have a strong effect on someone or something." (Miriam Webster) So, if our intention is to live the life we're called to live in Christ, then the impression we need to make is that of Christ, so others see Him in us, in our words, our actions and our deeds. If we're supposed to make an impact then it means we must pray that the impression we leave is a good one; a lasting one; a Christ-like, positive one.

Our hopes and prayers should be that, whether it's a family member, friend or a stranger we're dealing with, that we distinctly work to be about Christ in our actions and reactions. We should strive to make an impact on a world that is hurting, lost and crying out for the kind of love that only comes through Jesus Christ.

Woman of God, stand firm:

- Repeat to yourself that you are a bringer of God's love. You were made to reflect God's love to a hurting and fallen world. We are ones, being in Christ Jesus, who are able to reflect the love of Christ so that a world that is lost and hurting is able to see Him in us. Pray for others to see Him as you work to make sure that what you reflect is true, right and loving. Pray that you're obedient in how you follow His call and that you are able to make an impact merely because you know who you are, whose you are and because you are standing firm!

TAKE COURAGE AND STAND FIRM

I'd love to say that it doesn't take courage to say "yes" to who God calls you to be and stand firm in this battle against your very identity, but that would be a lie. It can be especially difficult if you've spent years tying your identity to someone else, or to a title or to the way you look. Bad habits and worldly thinking can only be challenged with the truth and that truth will set you free. However, sometimes standing in the face of the lies that held you to an image of who you thought you were or even to something you labeled yourself as, takes courage.

Let's face it, once your family and friends label you as something, they expect you to be that thing or that person they labeled you as. Hopefully you have supportive family and friends who see the best in you and want the best for you. Hopefully as you embrace who the Lord tells you that you are, stripping away the old and embracing the new, you will be encouraged and strengthened by those around you. However, realistically, not everyone has that kind of support and it can make embracing who you are in the Lord, even scarier. No one wants rejection from their family or friends. No one desires to be judged when they make a change or they finally accept who the Lord says they are. But it happens.

It's not always easy to be obedient to what God calls you to do, especially in a world that can be hurtful. It can be frightening. Big things, little things and people's expectations of who they believe you to be, can hurt you, especially if you're walking around unsure of who you are and where you stand on moral and spiritual principles. So, there is no doubt that it takes a bit of courage here and there to do what God shows you to do. Sometimes we want our own way and we want to argue with Him. (Not that any of us women of God ever fight and fuss and fume over the path we're on, right?)

Sadly, I could write an article about my own past experiences. *5 ways to fight, fuss and argue with God -* or *10 alternative ways say 'I want it my way', without sounding like a baby.* Most of the time I believe my whining to God comes more out of fear than out of stubborn willfulness, although there is definitely a bit of that in there. Not sure about you but sometimes I fear the direction God calls me so I turn from it. If there's a task He calls me to do, a relationship He leads me to end, a new venture He places in front of me to go forth and explore, my knees knock, my nerves get frayed and I doubt if I am strong enough, good enough, gifted enough or courageous enough to handle whatever it is.

In the Bible though, **Deuteronomy 31:6** says, "Be strong and of good courage, do not fear nor be afraid of them; for the Lord your God, He is the One who goes with you. He will not leave you nor forsake you."

Have you ever watched the movie, The Wizard of Oz? I loved that movie when I was younger. Now as an adult I find the meaning of the movie more beautiful than when I was younger even though it's filled with fantasy figures that are sometimes bizarre, if not funny or adorable. When I was younger though, I was drawn to the Cowardly Lion. I felt as if I could relate to his character. I loved they way he rolled his "R's" when he sang, how he played with his own tail and used it to dry his tears and I loved how his voice when he sang. His character was just that to me, a character. But I also related to feeling like a coward.

At a very young age I began to have moments of

stifling fear. I would be afraid to go to sleep at night for fear I'd awake and my whole family would be dead. I was afraid to be alone, to be in crowds, to hurt other people in anyway what-so-ever. I was afraid of germs, of displeasing someone else, of being not good enough or smart enough. Fueled by this fear I started a quest to be as perfect as I could be; to not make any mistakes, if at all possible. I not only became a perfectionist, but I became immersed in Obsessive Compulsive actions that ruled my life for many years. I truly saw myself as the Cowardly Lion. I took on the label my siblings gave me of "Miss Perfect". Even though it hurt to be called that, because they weren't complimenting me, they were mocking me, I felt I deserved it. For many years, what I labeled myself and what I allowed others to label me, became my identity.

It wasn't until I was in my early 30's that I discovered that I was not a label. I was not and never would be perfect and I was not a coward. I was your average, everyday woman who had no idea who she was and I needed a savior. While I was delivered from OCD, praise the Lord, it still took courage for me to step out and become who the Lord was calling me to be. I was a child of God but within that identity I was also a servant, a disciple, an evangelist, a woman who longed to live a life after the Lord, on the path He had for me and to be unashamed in doing so. While it took years for me to allow Him to truly mold and shape me in His way, I relied on His strength and courage every step of the way. If at any point I felt myself slipping back into old patterns and negative thinking, I would remind myself by reading His Word and immersing myself in quotes like this one by Nelson Mandela: "I learned that courage was not the absence of fear but the triumph over it. The brave man is not he who does not feel afraid, but he who conquers that fear."

Conquering something means to, "gain mastery over it or to overcome something". (Miriam Webster) Yes, by relying on the Lord, I was and still am reminded that who He made me to be is someone who is more than a conqueror. While I am human and sometimes still have fear, He made it possible for me to overcome that fear, to throw down the label of a coward, and step out into a life of courage.

When I think back to the childhood movie that still entices many of us to view it when it comes on TV, I can still recall the lyrics to the song the Cowardly Lion sung.

"Courage! What makes a king out of a slave? Courage! What makes the flag on the mast to wave? Courage! What makes the elephant charge his tusk in the misty mist, or the dusky dusk? What makes the muskrat guard his musk? Courage! What makes the sphinx the seventh

wonder? Courage! What makes the dawn come up like thunder? Courage! What makes the Hottentot so hot? What puts the "ape" in apricot? What have they got that I ain't got? Courage!"

That is the song he sung, when the truth of it is, he had the courage inside him all along. The Cowardly Lion mixed up the idea of cowardess, or lack of courage, with feeling fearful.

The definition of courage is "the mental or moral strength to venture, persevere, and withstand danger, fear, or difficulty" (Miriam Webster). Wow, isn't that wonderful? Don't we have that messed up in today's culture? We think that being afraid is the same as cowardess or if we dare feel any fear, we have no courage. Courage is not the lack of fear. Conversely, our current world culture teaches people that doing anything we want, consequences be damned, is courageous. It teaches that we can be who we want; forget about who the Lord created us to be. But living that way isn't courageous. It does not make you an overcomer or a conqueror. It makes you a conformer, or one who conforms to the ways of the world. Do you believe you have mental and moral strength? Perhaps you do but do you use it to pursue things that are unholy, immoral, unkind and opposite of who the Lord is calling you to be and what He is leading you to do? Then, harsh to say perhaps but, guess what? You aren't courageous. You're reckless and careless and a conformer, not a conqueror.

To all who struggle with feeling cowardly, please let me repeat it for emphasis; courage is not the lack of fear. Courage is doing the right thing, the Godly thing, the loving thing, even IF you are afraid. Courage is learning to stand firm, even if you don't currently know how to stand firm. Perhaps you're afraid of ending up alone if you stand firm or fearful of ending up persecuted if you use the armor of God and walk your path of purpose as the person the Lord created you to be. Maybe you're afraid of being judged, of getting hurt, of being ridiculed and rejected because you stand firm in who the Lord made you to be. Are you afraid to fail and look like a fool, or worse yet feel like a fool? Afraid you're not good enough? Smart enough? Pretty enough?

If you answered yes to any of those questions, then you are not alone. I was once where you are now. I ask, in whose eyes are you afraid you will be judged? Is that thought fueling your fear? Do you fear family and friend's judgment more than the judgment of the Lord? Are you looking at yourself the way you think social media is or family or coworkers are? Or church members? Or are you looking at yourself in the mirror and being honest, not self-deprecating or insulting but real, honest, open, truthful. Because if you do that, then you'll know that even if you do fear, you can still seek the Lord for courage. And that pesky fear you feel, it will fade. Like all fear eventually does, it will go away. Typically fear fades but sometimes it will be gone in the blink of an eye, especially when you replace fear with truth. Once the lies of fear have the light of truth shine on them, the fear completely disappears.

That's what the Cowardly Lion did. He saw the truth. The Wizard pointed out the facts to him, just like he did to the scarecrow and the tin man and to Dorothy. Because fear comes from lies and once you know the truth, the fear disappears and can no longer control you or who you are.

Don't forget what **Deuteronomy 31:6** says about being strong and courageous. I share it because I know this scripture to be true with all my heart. Courage is no small thing. The word courage or courageous is referenced over 120 times in the Bible and we're told 33 different times to "be strong and courageous." Even if it's a small thing we need courage to do, if it's of the Lord, He will give us the courage to do it. Whether you're afraid to dance in a crowd, sing in a choir, start your own business, record a podcast, confront a liar, cut someone out of your life, accept yourself for who you truly are, break off an unhealthy relationship, apply for a new job, report someone for abuse, sign up to serve in the armed forces, seek help for an addiction, go back to school, run into a fire, stick up for a classmate, volunteer your time, give away your money, babysit for a friend who has 18 kids with ADHD...He can prepare you for it all and fill you with the courage you need for whatever He calls you to do.

Woman of God, stand firm:

- Seek courage from the Lord through prayer and meditation on His Word, that your identity in Him will be affirmed, not destroyed by fear.

- Pray for the Lord to help you walk in the knowledge of who you are, making decisions for your life accordingly, out of courage and not fear. Standing firm and using the armor of God is no small thing. He will give you the courage to stand and stand firm when you seek Him with all your heart. Woman of God, do not forget that He will give you the courage and the strength to choose the armor He blesses you with in this battle.

- Write this scripture down on a piece of paper, an index card or on a note in your phone so you have at hand when you need it. **Joshua 1:9**: "Be strong and courageous.

Do not be afraid; The Lord your God will be with you WHEREEVER you go."

THE BATTLE CRY

Like no other time in history, the role of a woman in society, in the family, workplace and even in some churches, has never been more convoluted, confusing and devalued. The only place I have consistently felt valued, been truly known, and not alone, was in the presence of the Lord. In His presence I learned who I was, who He was to me and how much more beautiful and rich each day can be, standing firm in my faith and armored up so that I might be able to walk out His purpose for my life. I accepted a battle cry. That cry helped me attain the knowledge, protection and provision to become the best authentic woman of God I could be for my family and friends. That process is a daily process, ever on-going, ever-growing and a daily quest because I cannot stand firm if I decide one day I want to drop my armor and sit down. I have taken up my armor and shall not be moved.

As you learn to stand firm, and you pour yourself out to the Lord, don't worry when tears come, because they will. Rest assured that crying when you get upset, frustrated, and angry or because you feel afraid is all a part of the way we women were made. Those tears are good. We were given tears for a reason. They help us process our emotions. It's therapeutic and cathartic to release those tears in the right time and at the right moments. It's important that every now and then, every woman, and every man for that matter, has a good cry. Don't you let anyone ever tell you differently. But there's another kind of cry that's helpful and productive. It's the battle cry.

What is a battle cry?

It is defined as a "shouted word, phrase, or sound used by a body of fighters before or in battle: or a slogan, catchphrase, or motto that is used especially to rally people to a cause or to rouse people to action" (Miriam Webster). If ever there was a battle cry for the church today, it must be Stand Firm.

Women of God, in sharing with you what's been on my heart and mind, and what's been stirring my soul for years, my hope and prayer is that I have issued to you a battle cry. For those of you who have yet to understand this, my hope and prayer is that through accepting and humbly embracing the truth of what the death, resurrection and return of Jesus Christ has done for each us, that you too can join the church in this battle by putting on the armor of God in order to fight against the battle for your identity.

Before I truly understood that I was not alone in what I was facing as a woman, I felt hopeless, helpless and confused. I had times when I didn't want to wake up the next day and look at myself in the mirror. I had times I just refused to look in the mirror except for the very little I absolutely had to. There were times I felt so guilty about the way I acted or the words that came out of my mouth and the thoughts that I had, that I was convinced there could never be any forgiveness for me. I believed the lies that Satan told me and I worked hard to live up to the expectations of what the world said a successful woman is supposed to be.

One day I got to a point in my life that I felt as if I could cry no more. I felt as if all the tears I could ever muster up we're gone because, my goodness, who could cry more than I had? I felt like I was a constant weeping mess for so long that suddenly my tears dried up. I was becoming cold and callous. But it's because I was lost. I didn't know who I was. Yes, I believed in the Lord and yes, I'd studied the Word of God. I even got a Bachelor's in Theology and a Master's in Divinity. So, I knew the Word of God. I knew about the armor of God. But what I didn't know was that using it also applied to the fight for my identity. I truly had no idea that I was in the battle of my life, with a war being waged against my identity as a woman of God.

I was so tired of feeling like I had no idea who I was, being confused by what culture and society said I should be: be this one minute, that another minute. What my own emotions and feelings were telling me was contrary to what the Word of God said because I had believed the lies. I got to the place that all I wanted to do was give up. I went for a time not caring if I spoke to anyone; not caring how I looked, how much or how little I ate or if I took care of myself, because after all, I could never meet the standards of what the world said I should be anyhow. What was the point in trying? I became someone I was never meant to be, so there wasn't any way I could serve the Lord. In the process of trying to please so many other people and be who they thought I should be for them, I became hollow inside.

I could not be obedient to what God was calling me to do because I couldn't hear clearly from Him. I knew there was a call on my life, but I got to the point where it took all my energy just to go through the motions and take care of my family on a day to day basis. I felt stuck. I was afraid to move forward. I was afraid to look back. I was afraid to pray for guidance as to what step I should take next because I knew I wouldn't have the strength to make that step. I began to believe there was no way God would call me again to do big or small things, good or great things, because I wasn't good enough to represent Him. I wasn't smart enough. I wasn't talented enough. I wasn't strong enough. I didn't look the right way. I had made mistakes, took wrong turns, sunk into places of darkness that were not made for a woman of God. I didn't talk the right way, weigh what I should, eat like I should or have enough money in my bank account. Yep, that's right. I had bought into all those lies.

The day I finally understood that who I am is not dependent on who the world says I am, began as a very dark day and yet it turned out to be a day that shone the brightest light in to my life. It was a day a lifeline was thrown my way and the Lord revealed things to me I needed to know. That was the day that I sunk so low that I didn't think I was going to make it through the night to see the following morning. I had been alone because my husband was at work. We had a teenage special needs adopted son who was in a psychiatric hospital for having attempted to take his life, after assaulting me, yet again. My joints were dislocating regularly and my pain was out of control. My precious father had passed away. My husband and I were constantly arguing, living separately but in the same house. We were not in a good place. We'd had so much stress and so many hard times. I didn't have a job. My family was falling apart.

I hadn't prayed in a very long time because I stopped hearing from God. Why would He want to communicate with me anyhow? Turns out I couldn't hear Him because I was separated from Him out of my own disobedience. I had blocked Him out, out of shame, anger, rebellion, and because I spent more time trying to become something I was never meant to be than seeking who I was in Him. I wasn't living the way He called me to live. I had let the stress of life, what I thought were the needs of my flesh, my mind and my body, all take first place. I didn't know anymore what it meant to die to self. I no longer knew what it was like to push my own feelings up and out to pour them out at the foot of the cross. So, I had pushed them all deep inside where they screamed loudly at me every time I even attempted to pray. I sat alone at my house that night contemplating how many pills it would take for me to not have to wake up the next morning. I didn't want to live another day feeling that way.

At 11:03 p.m., I received a phone call. I didn't take it. I sent it to voicemail. That phone call was from a friend I hadn't seen in quite some time. I had gradually stopped putting effort into many friendships, sure that in a world that was crashing in around me, they wouldn't care if I stopped communicating. This friend had been out of the country for awhile on a mission and had no idea what I'd been going through because I'd stopped writing to her. I vaguely recalled she was supposed to be back in town at some point that month but didn't know when.

My friend left this message for me, "Karen, I know it's late but I just want you to know that as I sat here praying and reading my Bible, God has put you on my heart so strongly. He wants you to know that you are loved. Karen, go to 1 Corinthians 16:13. Read it. Memorize it. It says, "Be on your guard; stand firm in the faith; be courageous; be strong." Now is the time. He's been waiting for you to be courageous. He's been waiting for you to stand firm. You are loved. He is getting ready to do amazing things through you. Don't give up. Pray for God to reveal to you the hidden things. And stand firm. He loves you sister. So do I."

The tears I hadn't been able to shed for months, the ones I thought had all dried up, they came. Never before, even in my pit of despair and self-loathing, had I believed in coincidence and I still did not. I knew then and there that God was sending me a message through a friend, a woman of God, who was being faithful to do what the

Holy Spirit prompted her to do. So, I went to the other room, got a Bible and looked up the scripture. For the first time in months, I prayed. It felt strange, foreign. I had to push down the incessant thoughts that God didn't want to hear from me. I remembered the voicemail. This same friend had told me years before that if ever I was lacking vision, direction and wisdom that I should pray for God to reveal to me the hidden things and if I prayed in faith, believing He would show me, He would. I learned that I had to be prepared and rely on Him for strength because sometimes He showed me things about myself and others I didn't want to know but He always showed me what I needed to know.

That night, at 11:33 p.m., I prayed for **1 Corinthians 16:13** to be on my lips and in my heart. I prayed it out loud, over and over, until I was weeping. I prayed for God to reveal to me the hidden things as He helped me to stand firm and be courageous. God was faithful. He revealed to me the vast number of lies I had believed about who I was. He revealed to me that very night and in the days and weeks to come, how much of who I thought I was, was not truly who I am. He revealed to me how much of a people pleaser, world pacifier, diplomatic woman I had become. He revealed to me how little I stood up for myself, allowing everyone around me to be the priority rather than putting Him first and taking time to take care of myself in the process. He revealed to me that if I would walk with Him fully, not with one foot in the world and the other foot half-heartedly on the path He was calling me to; that I would be the woman I was made to be, learning to love myself and love Him all the more.

Through the journey God took me on from that day forward, I realized in my disobedience I had rolled over and let the enemy pummel me with lies and assault my mind until I was battered and worn out. Because of that, there may very well have been women just like me who had been waiting for me to do as God prompted my friend to do, as the Holy Spirit led her to do with me...reach out with the love of Christ and a message from His Word. A sister reached out to me in obedience and pulled me up off a ledge. I vowed then that I would learn to stand firm, be courageous and be the woman of God I was born to be so that I could reach other women with the saving message of Jesus Christ and who we are in Him.

I hope and pray that you too will stand firm. Let that be your battle cry. For yourself. For the woman God made you to be; or all the other women and men who are counting on you to be obedient to your call and obedient to do as the Holy Spirit prompts you to do.

Kill the comparisons before they kill you

Comparison is the internal action that's opposite of standing firm. When we compare ourselves to other people we're walking on shaky ground where it's possible to lose our footing. Comparison is a work of the enemy. It is a fiery arrow shot at every woman, causing many to stumble and fall as they try to become something they were never meant to be. Again, the enemy wants nothing more than for each of us to doubt who we are and become confused about who we're supposed to be and what we were made for. The enemy wants to steal your contentment, your joy, and make you feel like you're not worth loving unless you change things about yourself that you were never called to change. Comparing ourselves to others in and outside the Body of Christ is a faith killer and identity stealer.

In **Mark 12:28-31** it says, "[28] ...Of all the commandments, which is the most important?" [29] "The most important one," answered Jesus, "is this: 'Hear, O Israel: The Lord our God, the Lord is one. "Love the Lord your God with all your heart and with all your soul and with all your mind and with all your strength.[31] The second is this: 'Love your neighbor as yourself. There is no commandment greater than these."

How can we love a God if we believe that what He has made is junk? How can we love ourselves if we believe we were made in the image of a Creator who made mistakes when He created us? How can we love our God with all our heart, soul and mind if we think that who He made us to be is not lovable, not intelligent enough, not good enough or born in the wrong body? Yet women in the church every day proclaim they have a love for Him, all the while loathing themselves and believing that things would be better if they were different. Perhaps if their body was smaller, bigger, curvier, they could then love themselves. Perhaps if their breasts were larger, waist was smaller and hair was longer, like this person's or that person's, then they could love themselves. If they had a better job, more money, a husband who looked a certain way, then they could love themselves. Comparison has successfully been the killer of many marriages and the destroyer of many bodies that have been cut into, cut apart, lifted, reshaped, and for some, even distorted and irreparably mangled, all in a quest to become something that person was never born to be. We have forgotten what **Romans 12:2** tells us."[2] Do not conform to the pattern of this world, but be transformed by the renewing of your mind. Then you will be able to test and approve what God's will is - his good, pleasing and perfect will."

I believe this is what's at the core of the dismantling of many people's faith. We are

KAREN MCCRACKEN

conforming to the patterns of this world. Satan as sent a message to the world that our identities are up for grabs; that who we were born to be was a mistake, not purposeful and not planned. The message spreading like wildfire across the globe today is that God messed up; His ways are not perfect, none of us are worth loving the way we are and that life is not precious. With this message being flashed before our eyes daily via social media and entertainment, why would we ever believe that we should love ourselves?

At the very core of this commandment in **Mark 12**, we are told to love God and then love others as we love ourselves. Our world is in turmoil, hatred seeping into every aspect of our lives, because we love not. The world at large is wary of loving a God they've been told is imperfect. They are afraid to invest themselves in a church body that doesn't seem to love themselves yet alone love their neighbors. Sadly, there's truth in the statement that many in the church today do not love their neighbors as they should, but I contend that's because they've compared themselves with others, began a journey of self-loathing and hatred and so, they're doing what Mark 12 says, loving others the way they love themselves – loving them not. If we love others as much as we love ourselves yet all the while are growing to hate who we are, SO much so that we keep trying to change who we were born to be, then we actually love not.

How can we love ourselves in a world that pushes and pushes us to be something we're not? We must do as **Ephesians 6:11** says, "[11] Put on the full armor of God, so that you can take your stand against the devil's schemes."

We use the shield to deflect the lies and fiery arrows of the enemy. We put on the helmet of salvation to protect our brains; these little computers in our heads that hold the truth that we are sinners yet saved and we use it to protect our minds, declaring that our thoughts are not for the taking. We put on the belt of truth that we may discern what is a lie and what is truth so we will not be deceived and we then walk in that truth. We put on the breastplate of righteousness that we may have right thinking, right living and walk the walk God leads us to. We put on the shoes of the gospel of peace that we might walk in peace, in purpose and share the gospel message. We pick up the sword of the Spirit, which is the Word of God and know it so we can live it out. We live what the Word tells us; we write its truth on our hearts and minds and remember what God's Word says about who we are. We do as **Ephesians 6** and **1 Corinthians 16:13** tells us to. We stand firm.

Woman of God, what will your battle cry be?

Will you wait until you hit rock bottom, barely able to lift your head up, feeling as if you cannot face another day? Will you wait till you've spent year after year, changing who you are and how you look all in a quest to keep up with whomever you've been comparing yourself to? Will you wait till your marriage is on the brink of divorce? Till your unhealthy habits of binging and purging, has you wasting away to nothing? Or till you bury yourself in food obsessions until you have a heart attack? Will you wait until you can have one more affair on line? Or until you have one more plastic surgery and spend more money to alter who you are in the flesh? Will you wait until you can get high just one more time or until that last bottle of alcohol is empty? Or until you have time to clean up the lies you've told before they get even more out of hand? How far outside the Lord's plan for you and away from Him are you willing to roam before you look back and realize you aren't just tempted by the world any longer, you have become part of it, and you still have no idea who you are?

Please, let not a desperate cry of a weary soul be your only cry today. Let your cry be a battle cry. Pick up your armor and stand firm Woman of God. **Stand firm!**

I'd love to say that it doesn't take courage to say "yes" to who God calls you to be and stand firm in this battle against your very identity, but that would be a lie. It can be especially difficult if you've spent years tying your identity to someone else, or to a title or to the way you look. Bad habits and worldly thinking can only be challenged with the truth and that truth will set you free. However, sometimes standing in the face of the lies that held you to an image of who you thought you were or even to something you labeled yourself as, takes courage.

KAREN MCCRACKEN

ABOUT THE AUTHOR

Karen McCracken is a Christian Speaker and comedian who has spoken at over 350 women's conferences and retreats across the United States. She is an author and podcaster, hosting The Woman Inspired Podcast. Karen's passion is to reach women with the gospel message and to come along side women in the Body of Christ with the message of hope and truth for those who feel lonely, afraid and are drowning in an ever-changing, frightening world.

Karen is a wife, mom, avid gardener and loves the outdoors. She's handy in the kitchen, loves to dance while she does housework and enjoys making other people laugh.

To tune in to Karen's podcast, go to womaninspired.com or look for The Woman Inspired Podcast on your favorite podcast platform.

KAREN MCCRACKEN

WOMAN STAND FIRM

Made in the USA
Columbia, SC
15 August 2023

21596546R00102